Start a PAID Membership Website

Turn your passion into ongoing recurring income with your own subscription website

A n s e l   G o u g h

Publisher: MembershipSiteAdvisor.com
Project editor: Gloria Chauvin
Project editor: Janice Ayre

PRINTED IN THE UNITED STATES OF AMERICA

Additional resources:
www.MembershipSiteAdvisor.com

Disclaimer:

Contents

Free eVideo Offer
Watch us create a
Membership site
from scratch

Watch us create a membership site from scratch. We'll design our website, our "members only" page, put together exciting content and go live!

We'll create the ads, generate the traffic and sign-up free subscribers. You'll see us get our very first subscriber – in real-time! See it happen as we check our email.

Download your eVideo
Today

To download your eVideo simple go to the link below and enter in your name, email address, the place you purchased the book and your receipt number.

Visit:

www.MembershipSiteAdvisor.com/freevideo

About this book

This book is divided into 4 parts.

Part 1 will teach you how to conceive your membership site idea and confirm that it will be a profitable idea.

Part 2 takes you through the actual "nuts & bolts" techniques required to build a membership site from scratch. We'll discuss the software, web page design, and creating exclusive content.

Part 3 shows you how to start getting paying subscribers. You'll learn the latest Internet marketing strategies. The same strategies we have used to build very successful web businesses.

Part 4 our final section - shows you how to take your membership site to the next level, using advanced marketing techniques.

Enjoy turning your passion into ongoing recurring income!

Part I
Choosing a profitable
Membership site idea

CHAPTER 1

Test your Membership Idea in 15 minutes

"How to test your membership site idea in 15 minutes and possibly make a profit, before you even register a domain name."

Imagine spending hours and hours developing your membership site, writing articles, creating tools, setting up management software, etc only to find your idea doesn't work. Is there a way to test the profitability of your idea before you invest any time? There is, and we show you the steps we use to test ideas, and how to actually make a small profit (in most cases) while testing.

In your search to create a fun and profitable membership site, you've probably come up with many ideas. But how do you know which one will work? How do you know which one has the potential to be the most profitable idea?

Setting up a membership site requires some work (and a lot of time). We have a step-by-step system to determine if the idea will be profitable before we invest too much time into it.

Although there's no guarantee, these testing strategies can actually generate some cashflow before you even launch your membership site. Here's how we do it...

How to test your idea and potentially make a profit with 15 minutes of work.

Step #1: What is your idea?

For the purpose of this test we recommend you test several ideas at the same time. If you're short on ideas, you may want to take a look at www.subscriptionconnection.com for some ideas, or even just search your favorite topics on Google. Find out what's selling. Your philosophy should always be, "whatever they're buying (the people), I'm selling."

Step #2: Are there any similar products selling on the Internet?

If you already have your idea, make sure that you have searched the Net for similar products. You're looking for 2 things.

1. Are there products selling in this area? If so, this will help validate that a market exists.
2. Are there TOO many products selling in this market? If a market is too cluttered, it can be very costly to introduce a similar product due to promotional costs.

Take special note of Google ads (see page 160) that are running when doing your searches. Write down a few of the ads to get an idea or 'feel' for communicating to your market.

Try clicking on a few and looking at what's being sold. Does the site have a good traffic ranking (go to Alexa.com to check any site's traffic)? Is there anything unique about different sites? What headlines are being used in the Google ad and on the site?

Step #3: Join an affiliate program

Find a site that sells a similar product to your idea and that offers an affiliate program you can join. Ideally you'll choose a site that has good copy, a good design, testimonials and a good traffic ranking. Checking the traffic ranking can give you a rough idea if the product is selling or getting enough hits to make it viable.

Try to find an affiliate that pays at least 50%, although it's not entirely necessary. Normally you want an affiliate program to pay out as much as possible, but for the purpose of testing, it just helps cover your advertising costs when you make a sale.

Step #4: Are there similar products selling on ClickBank.com?

If so, are they ranked high on the list? The higher a product is ranked on ClickBank.com, the better sales it has. If it's a high selling product, then there's a good chance if your promotional activities are done right, you too will have a high selling product.

Step #5: Try to find an affiliate product where you feel you could write equal copy or better.

When selecting the affiliate product you are going to test market, you should aim to find something you feel you could match with your own product. This includes matching or bettering their sales copy. The reason is, you're looking to get similar results when you switch over to your own product.

Some other things to consider are - Can you get similar or better testimonials? Can you get similar or better premiums? Will your product be similar but unique - not a copy?

Step #6: Write a Google Ad.

Google Adwords gives you the ability to test an idea almost instantly. Recently a family member of mine considered starting a membership site on "Magic Tricks." To test the idea, before doing any work or registering a domain name, we wanted to make sure the idea would make money - or that the target market would be willing to purchase digital information on this topic.

With about 15 minutes worth of work we located a product on ClickBank.com and created our affiliate link.

We felt we could improve on both the site design and the sales copy.

We then wrote a Google ad, one that we could use when we bring out the new site. Here's a copy of the ad...

All **Magic** tricks revealed
Seen on TV. Learn every **magic trick**
in the book. Complete package. aff

We uploaded 101 Keywords. The hits started to come in and after spending $3.80, which equaled 76 hits (we normally only test with keywords set at 5 cents), we had our first affiliate order for about $49 - our commission $22.80. Not a bad ROI (return on investment) for a couple of minutes work.

Our next step is to test another ad and even try another magic product, just to give us a better understanding of the target market.

> **Tip:** Setting your keywords on minimum bid (5 cents) will also give you an idea of how competitive certain keywords are, and what you can expect to deal with when you launch your membership site. In the above example we found we could rank really well with just about every keyword. In fact, we got almost 300 hits within a few days. Think of what the traffic will be like when I upload 1,000 or 2,000 keywords instead of 101.

Step #7: Pick 100 keywords or more

To get decent results in a timely manner you'll need to run about 100 keywords. With just about any product you run, you'll notice that only about 20% or less of all the keywords you pick will pull any real results. The problem is, you don't know which 20%, so to cover most bases you'll need to upload 100 keywords.

> **Tip:** Check to see how many people are searching (using Overture.com's search term tool) on the top keywords you have selected. Anything over a few thousand indicates a potential viable market.

Step #8: Launch your campaign

We like to spend close to the 'break even' price of the affiliate program we are advertising. For example, if the affiliate product is selling for $49 and our commission is $22, we would look to spend around $10 - $15 to test the idea. We won't spend over the $22. If we haven't made a sale by then we cut our losses. Normally if you are promoting an affiliate program you won't want to just break even on the product -

unless it has recurring sales. However, we are just testing an idea here, so breaking even is fine.

Step #9: What is your conversion rate?

It's a good idea to track your conversion. For 2 reasons:

1. Different markets have different conversion rates. You need to know if you can make enough sales to cover your advertising and generate some cashflow.

2. When you launch your membership site, you can compare your conversion rate to your affiliate product's conversion rate. If it's lower, you will want to make some changes, if it's higher - congratulations, you're in business!

Step #10: Repeat the process with a different product idea

I'm always one for a back-up plan. It's always a good idea to test different ideas. By testing different topics you can narrow down which one will be most effective. For example, at the same time as testing the site on magic tricks, I also tested one on computer games.

We got lots of hits, almost 400, and not a single sale. The campaign bombed! Lucky we didn't spend days, weeks or even months developing a product in the same market as the affiliate product we tested.

Step #11: Create an ezine for your membership site

Now that you've been able to actually make some sales from your affiliate promotions, you can go ahead with confidence and create your membership site.

If you're running a content based membership site, you can do further testing by launching your website, but instead of selling a subscription, you offer visitors an ezine. This will allow you to test your sales copy and start building up a supply of articles for your members' only area.

Step #12: Modify your Google ad so that it points to your new site. Congratulations you're now in business!

To start generating traffic to your new site, just replace the URL link in the already tested Google ad.

Step #13: Email the customers from the previous affiliate sales and offer them a discounted subscription to your new membership site.

Now that you have your own site, you can email customers acquired through your affiliate promotions and offer them a discounted subscription to your site.

Be sure to remind them that they purchased xyz products from you and you thought they might be interested in your new site, and that's why you're offering them the discount.

Step #14: Monitor conversion rates

Is your conversion rate better, the same, or less than the affiliate program you were promoting? If it's less, then you need to find out why the product you were promoting before, got better results. Do they have a better offer, a better product, better testimonials, etc?

Keep playing around with your sales copy and offer until you can match or beat the affiliate product you were promoting.

Step # 15: Increase the number of keywords. Try to build up to at least 1000 keywords

Now it's time to start gearing things up. Start searching for more and more keywords to upload.

Use Google's and Overture's suggestion tool (found on their website). Take all the keywords that are pulling well and run them through the suggestion tools to generate new lists. Test keywords that are not entirely related to your subject, but may have common interests. For example, people searching under "dieting" may also be interested in "pedometers" or "exercise". So if you're marketing a product on diets, you'll want to target those additional keywords.

Step #16: Start running ezine ads and posting articles on discussion forums

We've been able to generate many sales simply by posting related articles on discussion forums. Start gathering a list of highly visited discussion forums and post comments and good quality articles on them.

Track down ezines (ezine-universe.com) and offer articles or simply run your tested ad in them.

Step #17: When you've replaced your income, quit your job. This is what I did!

So what are you waiting for? Find an affiliate program in your area of interest, write a Google ad and launch your membership site!

CHAPTER 2

How to use eBay as "LIVE" market research for your Membership Site idea

"eBay is one of only a few places that lets you see what people are spending their money on, in real-time. Here's how to use this 'live' information to create a membership site that has a motivated group of buyers."

W hy eBay? Before we answer that question, we have to look at what makes a product sell well? A hungry market! So to answer the initial question, "why eBay?..." because everyone on ebay is there for only two reasons:

1. To sell something.
2. To buy something. And the overwhelming majority is there to buy something!

What kind of membership site do you want to create? A membership site that has a "buying" market. You want to sell something that people are already actively searching for and buying.

One of the toughest questions most new membership site publishers have to answer (and even experienced membership site owners who want to launch another business), is: "What will be the topic of my new membership site venture?" Choosing the wrong topic can set you up for failure before you even run your first ad or attract your first visitor! Choosing the right topic can set you up for success even if you're not that good a marketer.

3 valuable marketing points exposed by eBay, every second

eBay lets you see, in real-time...

- Who's buying what

- How hungry they are for the product area or industry

- And what they're willing to pay

For example, check out the screen shot on the following page:

☐	86.71 ACRES REEVES COUNTY TEXAS CLOSE TO RED BLUFF LAKE AND NEW MEXICO BORDER	$6,100.00	34	1d 16h 52m
☐	300 Acres North Texas Land Cooke County Great Hunting	$3,000.00	●	23h 54m
☐	TEXAS WASTE BLUFF LAKE RESORT LOT Lake Whitney NR INCLUDES GOLF MEMBERSHIP	$2,000.00	1	7d 21h 00m
☐	GOV. TEXAS LAND 10 ACRES FABULOUS RANCH LAND INVEST	$1,800.00	12	3d 22h 49m
☐	Foreclosure Homes Throughout Texas and Louisiana Live On-Site Auctions: July 20th - July 30th	$1,000.00	●	1d 11h 26m
☐	18 ACRE HUDSPETH COUNTY TEXAS, LARGE, NO RESERVE!!! Invest in your future, build a ranch, 3 day NO RESERVE!!	$860.00	20	3d 01h 49m
☐	18 ACRE HUDSPETH COUNTY TEXAS, LARGE, NO RESERVE!!! Invest in your future, build a ranch, 3 day NO RESERVE	$665.00	17	5d 02h 25m
☐	GOV. TEXAS LAND 1/4 AC NICE GATED COMMUNITY INVEST	$560.00	19	3d 22h 49m
☐	40 Texas Style Acres in Beautiful Hudspeth County TX	$500.00	-	4d 23h 21m
☐	TEXAS 160 ACRES ..Hunt, Camp, 100% Financed to ALL, BUY! Surveyed! Recorded Access Easements.BUY USA LAND NOW!!	$395.00	-	6d 20h 46m
☐	TEXAS 160 ACRES - SURVEYED - RECORDED ACCESS CHEAP!!! Camp, Hunt, Enjoy ATV Friendly - BUY USA LAND NOW!	$395.00	-	5d 20h 46m
☐	Big Bend, Texas Land for sale in Lajitas!!! Mayor of resort, Clay Henry, benefits Terlingua School!	$355.00	3	21d 19h 10m
☐	WESTWOOD SHORES, TEXAS RESORT LOT Gated Private Country Club Community Golf	$295.00	-	4d 22h 34m
☐	TEXAS 160 ACRES, DIRT CHEAP PRICE - SURVEYED!!! Hunt, Camp, ATV Friendly - BUY USA LAND TODAY! FINANCED	$295.00	●	13d 23h 39m
☐	10 ACRE HUDSPETH COUNTY TEXAS, LARGE, NO RESERVE!!! Invest in your future, build a ranch, NO RESERVE	$277.50	8	6d 02h 04m
☐	LAKE GRANBURY, TEXAS Real Estate Cash Sale NO RESERVE ●	$211.00	24	3d 00h 19m

" Screen shot of people selling land.
Now this is an active target market. Take a look at how many of
the listings have bids - not to mention the number of bids, and
they still have several days to go. There will be some bidding
wars here! "

In a minute we'll break down each point and show you how to use this as your sure-fire research tool when choosing that all important topic. We'll also show you how to test the idea using eBay and Google before you spend days, weeks, months putting together a fully fledged operational member site.

What kind of target market do you need to identify on eBay?

1. People who are passionate about a topic or product: You will know if this is a passionate market by the number of products for sale and if there are a lot of bids on a high portion of the products for sale.

2. Bidders who don't seem to be able to get enough of the product. They want more and more. The bids are fast moving. There is a lot of activity amongst bidders.

3. Bidders who are spending good money. If most of the bids are around $2 then you may not want to sell to this market. It's too hard to generate an income on low end products. But if they are $40, $90, $2,000, etc, you know this market has money to spend on their passion.

4. Buyers who "cluster" in other areas online, not just ebay. You have to be able to reach this market in other ways, just not ebay. More on this later...

5. Frenzy bidders. Make sure that this market is addicted to the products. How do you know - just look at how aggressive the bidders are.

By using eBay as your market research tool, you are identifying markets and people who are showing you what they want to buy. They're showing you with their money! All you have to do is sell to them, what they are already actively buying.

How to use eBay as your live research tool step-by-step

Step #1: Look for eBay stores

Search through the categories until you find one you like. As mentioned before, you want to find products and categories on eBay that have a lot of activity. There should be a lot of products and a lot of bidding going on. Especially bidding wars on many different listings.

Once you find a category or target market that matches this profile, your next step is to further validate your research by checking out some of the sellers. Check to see if they have an eBay store (to do this simply click on some of the product listings and if the seller has a store, a link on their page will invite you to view additional products).

You are looking for eBay stores that are moving products in the same or related area. How do you know if they are moving products? Just check their other listings to see if they have bids on them.

Checking out eBay stores will give you a good idea if this is a hot market. Markets that aren't hot usually don't have sellers with successful eBay stores.

Tip: You can also search directly on eBaby stores by choosing that category on eBay's home page.

Step #2: Search on Google

After you find a product category that qualifies (using the information above), search for the product on Google. You are looking for 2 things.

1. You want to make sure there are a number of Google Ads running. This will help you further identify your market and spark ideas for advertising copy and other products that are being sold to this market.
2. If there are very few or no Google Ads, you may want to rethink your target market, as it may be too small to justify a membership site. If so, just start at step one again.

Step #3: Search on Overture's keyword suggestion tool

Finally, do a search on Overture's search term suggestion tool to roughly estimate the number of people searching for the topic on which you are about to create a membership site. Anything over 2,000 - 3,000 searches a month is good.

Step #4: Creating your test product

The easiest and fastest way to test a product or membership site idea is to do one of 2 things. 1. Sell an affiliate product. 2. Set up a simple website with some short copy on it and a "request for more information" form, in other words an opt-in form. You want to collect names and email addresses.

Number 2 is a great way to test an idea. Especially if your membership site idea is very unique compared to other products on the market.

We used this idea to launch our very first membership site and had over 400 people register their interest within days. All we were doing was collecting leads from a short one page website.

Our next step was to build the entire membership site and email those 400 + leads. Well that's exactly what we did, and we converted a huge percentage of them - we had more than a 40% conversion rate, and by then the list was growing daily!

It's important to note that we kept the list of enthusiastic leads excited by sending out updates and information on when the membership site would actually be launched.

Step #5: Search for forums and discussion groups:

Once you've narrowed down your target market, try searching for forums (just type the topic and the forum into Google - or go to Google Groups). Once again you are looking for activity from your target market. You want to see if they "get together online" and talk about their passion. Study the posts. What are they talking about? What are they having problems with? Can you provide a solution to common topics that are raised on the forum?

Locating forums will not only give you insight into what your targets want, but it will also give you a marketing resource which you can use to attract targeted traffic. You will be able to answer posts and post articles, providing you with a never-ending source of highly targeted leads.

Just do it

Test it out! Research a category on eBay. Check out the bidding activity. Check for eBay stores. Search on Google, search keywords, and check out some forums. Then go ahead and set up a simple website that collects leads. Finally set up some Google ads. Stand back and see what happens!

It will cost you almost nothing to set it up and test it out. If it doesn't work, you have wasted minimal time and very little money.

Real-life example: See what we taught put into practice in this factual case study

In the last article we explained how ebay can be used as a "live" research tool for developing membership sites topics (or any product for that matter). This report will show you how we actually implemented the techniques with a real-life example. You see how we used eBay to zone in our target market, how we arranged the test product, the steps we took to develop a landing page (test website), and our initial marketing activities (which started generating leads and interested buyers minutes after the site was uploaded).

We also share the exciting results of our Membership Site test, and where we go from here (and it looks like we are about to turn this example into a real-life membership site).

Have you ever had an idea for a membership site or product, but didn't know how to test it without investing a lot of work? We're going to show you how easy it really can be.

Step-by-step: From eBay research to a functional test membership site all within 24 hours

Step 1 - Searching eBay categories:

We started off by searching topics we were interested in on eBay. After searching many different topics, we noticed that there are a lot of people on eBay searching for established businesses to buy. Jackpot! We decided that would make a great membership site! There are constantly lots of bids and activity going on in this category - "web businesses for sale".

Two questions you need to keep in the back of your mind when scanning the bids and categories are:

1. Would this target market buy information (or in this case, a subscription to a membership site) about this product?
2. Is there enough information to justify frequent - even weekly updates?

Finally you need to pick something you are excited about.

For some time I've been interested in buying established businesses. On the following page is a screen shot of the category we became excited about.

Take a look at the number of bids on this page. Talk about a frenzy...! Does this look like an active market to you? There are hundreds of bids in this category. Everyone wants to buy an established business. But more importantly, look at what they are willing to pay... $750, $119, $305.... the list goes on. We saw one listing with many bids at $52,000! This market has money. Do you think they would be willing to pay for information that might help them make a better buying decision and avoid a costly mistake?

Step 2 - Searching for competitors:

Our next step was to check out the competition, not so much to find out if there were too many, but to make sure other people were having success selling to this market. We were excited to find many great products on the topic of buying a business.

One of the best tests you can do, is on yourself. Try and find a competitor's product that you really want to buy. When you find it, you can start to model some of their success and create your own unique angle. You're looking for that "a-ha" product.

Following is a screen shot of products advertised in this industry:

There are a lot of Google Ads, which is a good sign that products are selling well in this area. If there are no ads running, it could possibly mean this market is not viable. On the other hand if there aren't too many ads then it's going to cost me a fortune to generate traffic. In fact, minutes after launching our test website, we started getting leads for 5 cents a click.

<u>Step 3 - Selecting a test product:</u>

We always have 4 requirements when selecting a test product.

1. **Price:** The price has to be around the price point for which we want to market our products.

2. **Sales copy:** The sales copy has to be exciting, but not over hyped.

3. **Target market match:** The product has to match the exact same target market. This will also allow us to use this same product as a back end, and other joint venture activities between our businesses.

4. **Margin:** To keep our options open as a back-end product, we usually won't test with a product that has less than a 50% mark-up. Keeping a good margin will also allow you to make a profit on your test marketing campaigns, if successful.

Below is a copy of the course we found that met the above criteria.

Your Roadmap to Success

Step 4 - Setting up a landing page:

Designing a website can take a lot of work, and it's probably not a good idea to invest a lot of time into something that you're "just testing". With this in mind, we tend to use templates. This allows us to create a professional looking landing page (website) within a couple of hours.

In this particular example our landing page is designed to do one thing... collect leads (name and email address)!

We used the template to create a one page website. Visitors only have 3 choices when they visit the site. 1. Leave. 2. Enter their details. 3. Click on our "Contact us" link and ask a question. That's it!

Below is a screen shot of the template we used and how we modified it to create our landing page.

Template

Landing page

We used the copy and graphics from an established business selling a course on the topic we wanted to promote. This of course was done with their permission. We will go on to sell their product as part of our test. If all goes well, we will probably continue to sell the course and launch a membership site on the same subject as a back end product.

Step 5 - Launching our online ads

The obvious choice would be to run an eBay ad to start promoting the course, however we decided to test the ad copy using Google Adwords. Why? Because this allows us to tweak the sales copy and receive instant feedback.

Below are a couple of the ads we are using to test the idea.

Sample Google ads

Buy Est. Businesses
Congratulations, You're About To
Become A Business Buying Expert aff
www.MembershipSiteAdvisor.com

Buy an Est. Business
Literally "buy your income." How to
get sellers to finance purchase
www.MembershipSiteAdvisor.com

Our landing page immediately started generating leads. In fact, moments after launching our test campaign we had someone wanting to purchase the course (we weren't even set up to take orders yet!).

The landing page continued to generate leads throughout the day. Once we have a 'control' ad (one that generates the highest response), we'll launch a series of eBaby ads.

Where to from here?

We'll continue to generate leads and sales for the affiliate course while we design the actual membership site.

Our final step will be to move the membership site into the front line and sell the course as a back-end product to subscribers.

To check out our landing page go to:
www.BuyingSmallBusinesses.com

Real-Life Case Study #1

Rare "400-year-old Japanese investing technique" turns into a $20,000 a month Membership Site

"The membership subscriptions alone bring in about $20,000 a month and the product sales bring in an additional $2,000 to $3,000 a month"

3 years ago Daryl Thompson partnered with a unique investment expert to turn a 400-year old charting system into a hugely successful membership site. Daryl reveals his web business's success - from idea, to conception, to cashflow:

1. Daryl, before we get started can you tell us a little bit about your background?

I was born in Montgomery, AL and was raised in Mobile, AL. I attended the University of Oklahoma and got a B.Sc. degree in Mathematics. I then spent the next 28 years in Information Technology, mostly as a Programmer Analyst, with 5 years in managing an IT shop.

I spent 13 years with two different major oil companies, living in Chicago, Beaumont, TX and Houston. I then spent 15 years with a prestigious investment counseling firm in Houston. In February 2003, I was able to "retire" from the corporate world because of the Internet and our Candlestick Forum membership website.

I am married to my wife Barbara, have one daughter, Stacy and a toy poodle named Winston.

2. Could you give our readers some background on what CandleStickForum.com is all about?

CandleStickForum.com is an investment education site. Specifically, we teach traders in the stock, commodity, futures and options markets how to use the ancient art of Japanese Candlesticks, a 400-year old charting system that created legendary wealth for its inventors, to find market beating trades on a daily basis.

3. How did the idea for CandleStickForum.com come about?

My business partner and I met in our church Sunday School class. At the time I was still employed at the investment counseling firm in Houston. My business partner, Stephen Bigalow is one of the world's foremost experts on Japanese Candlesticks and has written one of the best books on the subject, "Profitable Candlestick Trading".

I was familiar with Japanese Candlesticks myself and was aware of the other main "players" in the area. I also immediately saw what our USP (Unique Selling Proposition) could be.

It seemed to me that the other major players in the area were trying to keep the subject of how to use Japanese Candlesticks successfully a "deep, dark secret". Most investors will say something like "I have heard about Japanese Candlesticks, but I just don't understand how to use them". After talking to Steve, I sensed that he had a very simple system on using the technique successfully. So that was our USP, taking this esoteric, secretive system and making it easy to understand and profit by it.

I told Steve I would do all the work in getting the site up and running for free, and handle all the maintenance after that, if we agreed to split all the profits after expenses 50/50. Thus CandleStickForum.com was born.

4. How many subscribers do you have?

We are currently maintaining around 200 members. We are scheduling some improvements to the site, and expect another 100 members or so when those improvements are complete.

5. Can you give us an idea on the kind of revenue that you generate from your membership site?

We sell educational material in the form of books, e-books, flash cards, wall posters, etc. in addition to the membership site. The membership subscriptions alone bring in about $20,000 a month, and the product sales bring in an additional $2,000 to $3,000 a month.

6. How long have you been running the business? And how long did it take before you first started yielding a profit?

We have been "officially" running the business now for about three years. I worked on the site after hours and weekends for almost a year before that, kind of "figuring things out" as we went along.

Our site has gone through two major revisions from the first version. We now have to laugh as we look back in the archives at that first version. Still, those primitive versions of the site were producing more and more income every month.

Most experts will say don't expect much income for about six months after launching a site. I think that depends on what you have to offer.

There was a lot of demand for what we have and we started producing nice income about three or four months after the "official" launch date. Keep in mind though, that Steve had "instant credibility" since he had his book published by that time.

I still remember our jubilation when we signed up our first member, then our first 10, then our first 50. It is really gratifying to see people willing to spend their hard-earned money on what you have to offer!

7. Who is your target market?

Our target market is basically anyone who wants to be able to understand how to use Japanese Candlesticks to successfully trade the markets.

8. How do you find and advertise to your target market?

Our most successful techniques have been search engine optimization and producing a free ezine, and combining the two techniques.

After about three months, the search engines started picking up on some of our main terms, like "Japanese candlesticks" and "candlestick trading". We provided lots of content around those terms, so we got ranked very high, either first, second or third for our main keyword phrases in Google.

We then researched other keyword phrases in WordTracker to see what people were actually searching for related to our products. We then put out a bi-weekly ezine, and optimized the ezine pages around the other search terms. We keep the ezines as HTML files on our site so the search engines will pick them up.

Also, the ezine itself almost always leads to new subscribers. We have an opt-in signup form on every page of our site, with a free report called "The Amazing Powers of Japanese Candlesticks" and a short autoresponder series going out to all the new ezine subscribers. We have built the opt-in list to around 5,000 subscribers.

We have been experimenting lately with Google AdWords, and are starting to see some results from that.

9. Where do most of your visitors come from? Search engines, pay-per-click, link exchanges, ezines, etc? List in order of importance.

I would have to say search engines, followed by producing our ezine.

10. Do you have many strategic alliances or joint ventures that bring high volume traffic? If so, how do you go about

putting together a joint venture? What do you say to get a potential partner interested?

This is an area that we have thought about and need to work on in the future. But the joint ventures we have done so far have actually been initiated by people approaching us, not the other way around. I think that comes from the "instant credibility" factor of Steve being a published author by a well-known publishing house.

But in general, to get a potential partner interested in a joint venture, you must be sincere and state specifically WHY you think the joint venture would work and WHY the joint venture would be a win-win scenario. Try to make the joint venture as much a "no-brainer" as possible for the other person. I think it is as simple as that.

11. Are there any other promotions that you have found to be effective in bringing you paid subscribers?

As mentioned above, we have "played around" with Google AdWords. I think a much more scientific (strategic) approach to that technique will benefit us in the future. We are also working on setting up link exchanges with similar sites to ours.

12. Have you tested various pricing to find the best combination?

To be honest, we really have not. One of our plans in the future is to have multiple levels of membership. We need a low-end for people just wanting to "test the waters" and get the basic information, an intermediate level for those having the basic knowledge and wanting to go to the next step, and then an advanced level for the "players". Ours is basically an "all or nothing" solution, which I am sure has cost us some income over the long run.

13. How would you go about building the business, getting more subscribers?

- The first thing we would do (and plan to do) is to add more benefits and services for the members, while keeping the subscription fee the same. I think that in business, you have to constantly "astonish" your customers to keep their interest levels high.

- We will also just keep doing what is working now, which is to continue to add useful content so the search engines will pick up more of our search terms.

- We will spend more time and effort testing Google AdWords.

- We will continue to look for suitable link exchange partners.

- We also are constantly on the lookout for ways to automate the business processes, or to "farm out" some of these processes so we can focus on the income-producing activities, as well as our core competencies to provide more and more useful information to our members.

14. As you know, successful businesses usually work off some kind of system. How would you describe the system you have in place? For example: Lead acquisition, following-up with the lead, how you convert the lead, how you retain a new subscriber?

Our basic business model is lead acquisition via the free report and ezine signup, followed by a series of autoresponder emails to entice the prospective member to subscribe. To be honest, this part of the process may be our "weakest link" in the business model. There is much more we could do to strengthen the email autoresponder follow-up.

As far as retaining members, we always follow up with those who have cancelled to understand why they cancelled, and based on their answers, try to come up with some kind of offer to have them stay on as members.

15. How is your retention? Is there anything that you do in particular to keep subscribers coming back and renewing or keeping their subscriptions?

Our studies have indicated that, if we can keep someone on as a member for four months or longer, then they are good candidates to become long-term subscribers. We have many people drop off after a month, since we have a very generous money-back guarantee during the first month.

Also, our business is affected by the stock market. It seems when the market turns down, even though we show people how to make money even in a down market, we lose subscribers. I think that just reflects the bad mood in general of most investors in a down market.

We have talked about a member-retention program, but have not implemented it yet. But our plans call for additional benefits to longer-term subscribers, more products for free or at a reduced rate, reduced membership fees, etc.

16. What kind of strategy do you use to separate yourself from your competitors?

I think most of our competitors are in a "pay me first, then I will tell you what I know" mode. In contrast, we provide lots of useful information for free on our site. Also, our USP of "keeping Japanese Candlesticks simple" separates us from our competitors.

17. Do subscribers receive any other additional services?

Our subscribers receive free of charge most of the products we have for sale on the site. They also enjoy greatly reduced rates to our live seminars.

18. What have you found to be the best way to convert traffic into paying customers?

Our free ezines, by far. I think the feeling is that "If we are getting this for free, what can I get as a member?".

19. What kind of conversion rate do you have for your site? (Unique visitors to paying customers)

I will assume you mean by "paying customers" new members, since we have many other products for sale at different price points on the site. This is yet another area that we could greatly improve on. Our conversion rate is very small, around 0.002, but fortunately our price model is such that we don't need a lot of unique visitors each day to support the business. But again, we definitely need to improve on that conversion ratio.

20. Do you operate or plan on starting other membership sites?

Absolutely! The membership site model is what provided me with the opportunity to leave the corporate rat race at a relatively young age. The recurring income from membership sites is crucial. If we had to rely on the income solely from product sales, I would still be sitting at my desk in my old job.

TradeAndGrowRich.com will be my own site. It will be based on the timeless success principles from Napoleon Hill's great book, "Think And Grow Rich", but will apply specifically to trading the markets.

21. Can you tell us a little bit about TradeAndGrowRich.com?

I have spent the last 16 years studying and successfully applying what really works in stock market investing. This has allowed me the privilege of being ranked in the top 10% of the U. S. population in terms of net worth.

With Trade And Grow Rich, I hope to help many other investors quickly learn the systems and techniques to actually become wealthy, not just earn a living, trading the markets. I will also feature experts in other areas, such as E-mini futures trading, Forex trading, other stock market professionals, etc. to show our members how to be successful in those markets.

22. What will be your first steps in launching this new membership site?

I am working on a publicity campaign to launch the site. This will be comprised of press releases mainly, but I am also investigating several other avenues of free and low-cost publicity.

1. I will definitely start a "Trade And Grow Rich" ezine to entice prospective subscribers to sign up.

2. I will develop a series of autoresponder emails to accomplish the same objective.

3. I will work on a Google AdWords campaign and have it ready to test.

23. Where will be the first place you promote the site to start getting subscribers?

I will place a press release at www.prweb.com .

24. What would be the most important thing you would say to someone trying to start and promote his own membership site?

Well, I want to help out as much as possible, so I would like to say several things, mainly based on our experience, including the (many!) mistakes we have made.

I think the first thing I would say is to definitely find and use some sort of membership site software. Otherwise you will be facing a nightmare of membership maintenance issues, which will consume most and eventually all of your time.

The second thing I would say is to always think "under-promise and over-deliver". Things always take much longer to implement than you think they will.

The third thing I would say is, "don't think you have to have all this figured out before you launch the site!" You will find the answers to many of your questions by necessity when you have a real, live site on your hands! Also, there are many membership site owners out there, myself included, who are willing to help you get started.

Finally, I would say "Just Do It!" There are hundreds, if not thousands, of people out there who are willing to pay for what you have to offer. Never sell yourself short, or take for granted your area of expertise. Remember, you do not have to be "The World's Expert" on something. You just have to know a little more than most of the people out there. And as you can see above, we are doing a FEW things right, and A LOT of things wrong or not as good as they could be, and we created a very successful business in just a few months.

So go for it!

- J. Daryl Thompson

* We would like to thank Daryl for the information and insights he has shared. Daryl is the CEO of Trade And Grow Rich LLC, and is also a subscriber to MembershipSiteAdvisor.com

CHAPTER 3

Top 10 Membership Site ideas you can start today

Want to start a membership site, but not sure what topic to pick? Our research uncovers the top 10 Membership Sites you can launch. Includes a breakdown and marketing statistics on each one.

They say there are 2 kinds of entrepreneurs. 1. A pioneer - one who loves to always start on a new project. 2. A settler - one who likes to stick with what he's doing. Which one are you?

I'm a pioneer. I love to start a new project and then another and another. I've always got several going at once. In doing so, I'm always watching niche markets and looking at what sells.

I do this simply because there are only two ways to sell, 'push or pull'. Which is better?

Imagine two business owners. Both open a shop across the road from each other. Business owner 1 decides to sell a brand new product. Although it's a great product, no one's ever heard of it, and it takes a bit to explain. He starts a massive advertising campaign to educate potential customers.

Business owner 2 decides to sell a relatively new product. However, a lot of people have read about it in magazines and newspapers. They are looking where to purchase it.

The first business owner was using the 'push' method, the second business owner was using the 'pull' method. The 'pull' method will always have a short sales cycle and a higher conversion rate. Potential customers are already searching for it.

You can either chase people and tell them about your new product or service, or you can have them come knocking on your door saying... "I'm looking to buy this widget".... Which business owner would you rather be?

With that in mind I'm about to share 10 membership site ideas that I believe fall into the lucrative 'pull method' market.

Industry areas to choose from

- Business Tools

- Finance

- Hobbyist sites

- Self Improvement

- Wellness & Health

- Career advancement

- Entertainment

- Home and family

- Self protection

- Travel

Why visitors become subscribers

Everyone has hot buttons or 'motives' for buying. Every 'motive' falls into one of these 5 categories:

Gain: Visitors want to gain some kind of advantage, whether financial or personal, from becoming a subscriber to your site.

Pain: Visitors want to avoid some kind of pain, or prevent something from happening - like losing assets, or their health (the wellness industry).

Pleasure/Entertainment: They want to download their favorite music file, meet someone online (dating sites), improve their sex life, etc.

Doom & Gloom: They are scared of getting sick by drinking unfiltered water, or they buy protective gear in case of a terrorist attack... Something has scared them into purchasing.

Controversy: Visitors want to become subscribers so that they can read the latest gossip, or to learn about a theory or practice that others may disagree with, etc.

What 'motives' does your membership site or idea fall under?

A word of warning

Use caution when publishing any information relating to finance. To do so can sometimes require licensing, and to not have a license can result in heavy fines.

When choosing a membership topic, make sure you do have the necessary experience to provide reliable and excellent content.

What if you don't have the experience, licenses, etc? You can always just be the publisher and interview those who do. I'm in the process of launching another membership site with a partner. The topic - independent film making. Neither of us has ever produced a film, however we have experts already lined up to be interviewed. There are always experts eager to be interviewed. Their motive is usually free publicity, the excitement of sharing their knowledge, or simply the honor of being asked.

We just become the publishers (reporters so to speak) - not the experts. What we do have is knowledge of the market and industry. That's all we need. In fact, experts are usually easy to find and exciting to interview. You can meet some pretty famous people and build a great network of powerful contacts.

The Top 10 Industries

Targeting an industry alone is hard. Targeting a niche within a certain industry is far easier. For this reason we have provided example ideas for each of the 10 industries.

Below is a breakdown of the above industries with corresponding marketing statistics to prove the validity of the idea.

#1 Business Tools

- This is a hot area, especially web-based applications. Web business owners usually have limited knowledge when it comes to setting up new applications, or making the back-end of a website work.

If you're technically savvy, consider designing a membership site that does the work for some particular job that provides a solution for the non-technical user.

Topics that might do well include:

- Automated email management for a specific industry

- Spam filters

- Automated order processing

- Affiliate management

Another example, my brother-in-law helps run a successful site that provides spam filtering for corporate subscribers.

Any service based membership site that provides web-based tools or applications that are wanted, would do very well.

Even if you're not technically savvy, you can always hire a programmer to do the work for you. Web based tools and applications can be designed for as little as a few hundred dollars using services like www.rentacoder.com and www.elance.com

Stats:

- The keyword "web tools" gets over 12,000 searches a month on Overture. A more defined niche keyword would probably have even more searches, or at least a more responsive market.

- Example Site: Bravenet.com boasts over 5 million members. This service based membership site provides all kinds of web based tools for the 'not so' technical web master.

#2 Finance

- Membership sites providing advice on real estate, stocks and financial planning consistently do well. This also includes sites that can show people how to become self-employed or launch their own business.

Topics that might do well include:

- How to invest in the stock market

- How to buy real estate

- How to start an ebay business

A combination of tools and advice/content, seem to be winners.

Stats:

- The keyword "real estate investment" gets over 22,000 searches a month on Overture.

Example Site: InvestmentHouse.com has over 130,000 free and paid subscribers and brings in over 2 million dollars a year.

#3 Hobbyist sites

- Hobbyist membership sites are starting to pop-up everywhere. The best way to pick a topic is to look at various articles in specific magazines.

Topics that might do well include:

- Digital video production

- Downloadable blueprints and plans for electronic gadgets

- Improve your fishing

- The best 4WD destination

- Improve your Golf in 7 days using our online instructors

- eVideo cookbook

- Create a self-sufficient home. Solar power, plans and blueprints for alternative energy, etc.

- Gardening

- Sports

Stats:

- The keyword "fishing vacation" gets over 41,000 searches a month on Overture. A possible market for a membership site on "The Best Fishing Vacation Destinations" - Members get coupons, inside information, reviews, discussion forums, video clips of the destinations, etc.

- Example Site: Rivals.com, providing the inside scoop on sporting events, sold over 75,000 subscriptions in under 2 years.

#4 Self Improvement

Topics that might do well include:

- Personal development

- Mastering French online

- Goal setting

- Public speaking

- Body language

- NLP (Neuro Linguistics Programming)

- How to win friends and influence people

- Time management

Stats:

- The keyword "human resource management," gets over 13,000 searches a month on Overture.

- Example Site: HRnext.com, a human resource site, sold over 3,000 subscriptions at $395 each (yearly subscription). They used a combination of viral marketing, Google Adwords and Overture.

#5 Wellness & Health

Topics that might do well include:

- Dieting - How to cook your favorite foods without the carbs

- Women's health

- Alternative treatments

- Dangerous foods

Stats:

- The keyword "low carb" gets over 25,000 searches a month on Overture.

- Example Site: eDiets.com, charges $10 a month and has attracted thousands of paying customers by running banner ad campaigns and joint ventures with brand name companies like Atkins.

#6 Career advancement

You can target many different industries, like builders, martial arts schools etc. However, a good place to start is with professionals. For example a friend of mine, who owns a chiropractic clinic, pays a lot of money to subscribe to a membership site that teaches him how to run his business more effectively. This site includes tested ads, direct mail pieces, how to effectively set up your clinic so you can see more clients in less time... you get the idea.

Topics that might do well include:

- How to get a pay rise every time

- How to improve your (whatever) business

- How to get your dream job

- The top 100 dream jobs

- How to live and work overseas

Stats:

- The keyword "career builder" gets over 79,000 searches a month on Overture. Once again this keyword could be narrowed down more, to reach the exact market.

- Example Site: EmploymentGuide.com. We don't know their number of subscribers but their excellent Alexa traffic ranking of 10,493 suggests a lot...

7 Entertainment

Topics that might do well include:

- Download the latest Music MP3 file (check legal issues)

- Download movies

- Online real-time computer games

- The keyword "online game" gets over 700,000 searches a month on Overture. A more defined niche keyword like "online RPG Game" still gets over 8,000 searches a month. The narrowed down keyword would be a far more responsive market.

- Example Site: EverQuest.com. A 3D online game played by hundreds of thousands of fans from around the world. They're making a fortune with subscriptions going for $10 a month.

#8 Home and family

Topics that might do well include:

- Do-it-yourself home improvements

- How to add $10,000 worth of value to your home for $700

- Gardening

- Raising kids

- Child birth

- Recipes

- Ancestry

Stats:

- The keyword "family history" gets over 36,000 searches a month on Overture.

- Example Site: MyFamily.com took 3 years to make $200,000. Now they get more than 100,000 new paid subscribers every quarter.

#9 Self protection

Topics that might do well include:

- Learn self defense online

- Forget about going to classes - attend a virtual training academy

- Rape safe

- How to protect yourself from air rage (violent passengers on a plane). There is actually a successful course running, that teaches air rage self defense to flight attendants. Did you know that the "Association of Flight Attendants" in the US, estimates 4,000 incidents of air rage each year? This course is not a membership site, but could be turned into one... www.gracieacademy.com/academy/gard.shtml

- How to prepare for disasters

- Food storage

- Emergency evacuation plans

- Business Protection

- Information protection. Eg: Computer data

Stats:

- The keyword "data protection" gets over 3,000 searches a month on Overture.

- Example Site: Xdrive.com provides secure online data storage for corporate clients.

#10 Travel

Topics that might do well include:

- How to live and work in Paris

- How to buy your airline tickets at travel agency prices

- How to fly for free - without using frequent flyer points

- Travel the world accommodation free (house sitting/swapping)

Stats:

- The keyword "paris tour" gets over 8,000 searches a month on Overture.

- Example Site: France-property-and-life.com, a perfect example of how to run a membership site on moving and living in another country.

One of the greatest secrets to success

I follow this rule every time I start a new project. I continually remind myself of this rule. Study it. Write it down. Imprint it into your brain. It's simply this...

"Find out what people are ALREADY buying and give it to them"

I hope these topics have sparked some ideas for you. Research your market, find out what they're already buying and then build a membership site around it. Success is a lot easier that way...!

Picking hot topics to launch a membership site

The majority of your membership's site success will depend on the topic you pick. Here's what's hot and how to pick a revenue producer...

So how do you know what topic to even start with? How do you know if your topic will be a winner? How do you know if there is a big enough market to support you full-time? How do you know if your market is willing to pay?

I'll give you the answer to all these questions with one word - "research." Although it's fair to mention here that a part of research should also include "testing."

Let's break each section down and learn how you can research and test a topic. But first...

How many subscribers do you need to replace your income?

It's not many! Let's crunch some numbers. If you charge $15 per month per subscriber, you only need 200 subscribers to better the average yearly income. If you target right, with the right message, you can reach that goal pretty quickly. We did better than that in about 6 months. And that was without spending a dime on advertising. It was all joint venture/viral marketing.

How to pick a starting topic?

Getting started. I find this the fun part. What topic do you want to get paid to research and write about? I like to choose something close to my heart so that my passion or excitement shows in my writing.

As soon as you decide what you're passionate about, you need to check the market. You might end up actually targeting a smaller niche within your overall market. You may not even know what that smaller market is yet. We'll help you find it.

How to find your niche associated with that topic

Ok, so you have a passion. What is it? Take a moment to think about that... Let's say martial arts. But we're not just going to launch a membership site on martial arts. We have to drill down. Start drilling down your topic. eg...

What kind of martial arts?

What does your market consider as "news?" (this is important... exciting news always draws attention/subscribers)

What questions are being asked in magazines on that topic?

What problem questions does your market ask?

What's being discussed on forums?

What questions on forums get the most "viewed hits?"

Find the most commonly asked question from the list above. The answer to this question will be your niche market.

We put this research to the test and found a number of membership sites offering news and information on champion fighters. What did we do next? A quick Alexa check showed these sites had traffic rankings of 100,000 or under. We just qualified this market as a good one.

Now confirm our findings, with a keyword search. Go to...

Overture Search Term (www.inventory.overture.com)

A number of searches revealed several keywords, that also matched up with the forum questions. Anything with 2,000 or more searches is considered a good market. Once again... that's what's hot... that will be our niche. We've drilled a topic down within a market. Remember we are not looking at the entire market. We want our niche. Now we know how to talk to our market, and what they want!

Do some research into what other sites are charging to sell books, videos, magazine subscriptions, membership sites (if any). If there seem to be lots of publications in circulation, then your potential market has money and is willing to pay. You're in business.

Testing: Joint venture market research

Contact other businesses you see selling the information. Ask a few non-intrusive questions. Example: Have you sold many copies of your book/video? During this friendly conversation you may even have the opportunity to set up a joint venture.

If you're unsure about contacting a company, you can always look around to see how many other companies are selling the same product. If there is a number of them, that will give you a good indication of a successful product.

Now all you have to decide is, if your topic is better as a service orientated membership, or content orientated. Is your membership more a service with tools etc., or more articles and case studies? Understanding your market will help you decide this. Choosing the right one can have a big impact on your success. For that very reason, we like to include a bit of both. But we will lead with one or the other.

Enjoy getting paid to research and write about your passion!

10 point check list for a successful membership site

Evaluation check list. How does your site match up? If you're not selling many or any subscriptions with your membership site - then you might be missing one of these 10 points. But get them right and you've probably got a winner.

Getting all the small and not so small points right can mean the difference between success or failure. It's these points that usually separate those who run a profitable membership site from those who struggle to get more than a handful of subscribers.

I consider all of these points before launching any new project.

10 point evaluation check list

#1: Are you selling what people are buying?

Sometimes I have people coming to me and saying I would like to sell this product, without having a good idea of the market, and what the market is already buying.

Your chance of success will be dramatically increased if you start off selling something that people are already buying.

#2 Do you know how your market thinks?

Not only is this necessary when introducing a new membership site, but to keep up with changes in the market you need to know and understand what your market is thinking. This is a dynamic thing. It keeps changing and evolving. What's popular now, might not be popular in 12 months.

If you know how your market thinks, you can quickly mould to any changes and even predict them before it happens.

#3 Do you know where to find your market?

Fortunately if you're publishing information on a topic you're passionate about, you will know where the market sources its information because you're one of them. In fact, this is one of the best ways to identify opportunities and "waves" in the markets.

#4 Do you know your competition?

If your competitor has a better product, with better marketing - you'd better improve the value of your product or add something unique. Your entire goal is to create happy customers. That usually means continual improvements and changes as your customers change and grow. Continue to make your customers happy and give them what they want, and you'll have a profitable and long-standing business.

#5 Can you summarize in one sentence why your membership site is better or different than another one on the market?

As soon as a potential subscriber visits your site, he needs to immediately identify what makes you different. This uniqueness should be publicized in your headline and throughout your copy.

Many times a simple (but sort-after premium) can give you the added advantage. The more unique and valuable your site, the more subscribers you'll acquire and keep.

#6 Do you know where to advertise?

Whether it's knowing which keywords to pick or which magazine to advertise in, you should have a good idea where to run promotions. As mentioned in question #3, 'knowing where to find your market' is one of the methods we use to identify a profitable opportunity. Many times this is how we find product ideas. We just look at where to advertise and what is repeatedly being promoted or talked about in that particular publication. It's as simple as this.

#7 Can you identify possible joint venture partners?

Locating joint venture partners (and also analyzing competitors) can give you an instant idea of market activity. For example, their Alexa traffic ranking. If it's high, then they may be good candidates to promote your membership site.

In the past, we've based an entire product just on one joint venture deal. But, we pitched the idea before we invested in the development time required for a new product. Knowing joint venture partners can help narrow down your market and even give you ideas for improvements, based upon your partner's feedback.

Joint venturing can also be used to add a partner's product to yours. For example, we've recently done this with the creators of **aMember Pro**.

#8 Is there a viral marketing element you can add?

It's far easier to build a viral marketing element into a product during creation, than it is to do it later. Try to find some way to have subscribers pass the information onto other possible subscribers. This usually means giving away something for free or creating some kind of 'buzz.'

We recently developed a marketing campaign that allowed current and potential subscribers to vote on a new product release. Voters can win a prize, and the more people you get to vote the more chance you have of winning. In this case, the viral marketing element is short term - but it will be well worth the massive exposure.

#9 What premiums can you add?

Consider this - what products will your subscriber have to buy anyway? If you can give this away as a free premium, you can double your conversion rate. For example, a membership site selling website templates could offer a clip art package as a premium.

Alternatively, you could offer something a subscriber would really want to buy anyway. For example, a membership site that offers web-based, dispatch software for service-call companies, could offer a free white paper or booklet on 'How Service Companies can Increase Billable Time'.

#10 Is there a growing market to support ongoing subscriptions?

1000 subscribers can generate a great income - even a few hundred will do in some cases. Although it may not seem like many, you may have to work through 20,000 - 40,000 leads just to get a thousand subscribers.

Recently a major VCR manufacturer announced they would no longer produce VCRs - as result of DVD recorders taking over the market. Would it make sense to now start a VCR manufacturing company?...

Does your membership site idea have a growing market?

How does your membership site or idea, stack up?

Compare your idea or your current membership site against this checklist and see if you can honestly tick off each question. If you can't, it may be that you have to go back to the drawing board or find out the answers to the questions.

Knowing what you're getting into beforehand can help save you costly mistakes and valuable time. Follow our checklist and get started in the right direction and watch your site grow.

Real-Life Case Study #2

Inside a million dollar a year membership site

Where does the owner of this million-dollar-a-year membership site focus his time? Where does he run his ads? How does he generate hundreds of thousands of visitors? Our exclusive interview reveals exactly how this health guru is doing it all from home

Global-fitness.com is an award-winning, results-based online fitness program. In addition to very effective customized exercise programs and diet plans, GHF offers online personal trainers. We go behind the scenes of this million-dollar membership site with Chad Tackett, founder and sole owner of Global-fitness.com

1. Chad, can you tell us a little bit about your background?

I have a degree in Exercise Science and Nutrition and am certified as a personal trainer.

2. Could you give our readers some background on what Global-fitness.com is all about? What does a subscriber receive?

Global Health & Fitness (GHF) is a members-only website designed to help you achieve all your fitness goals. Whether you are a beginner or advanced, GHF will help you avoid the common mistakes that waste your time, teach you techniques for making your routine much more effective and personally guide you step-by-step to achieving new results again and again!

GHF members receive personal fitness consulting, customized exercise programs, healthy recipes and meal plans, books and videos, fitness tracking software, and much more. GHF has made having your own fitness instructor, dietician and personal motivator affordable for almost everyone. We've been in business since April 1, 1997.

GHF Members receive...

- Unlimited fitness consulting via e-mail with a detailed response within 24 hours (365 days a year) - guaranteed!

- Highly effective exercise programs customized to your goals, fitness level and time and equipment availability.

- 175 exercise instructions and video demonstrations to view at home or print out and take to your health club or workout room.

- Protrack, our exercise and nutrition tracking software.

- The new GHF Training Manual and online books on each of the 5 Components of Optimal Health.

- Hundreds of delicious, healthy recipes and shopping lists!

- Weekly live chats with GHF's experts and members!

- FREE entry to the GHF Fitness Challenge, our 12-week fitness contest!

- Full access to the new members-only Fitness Forum where you can get expert advice, as well as correspond with other members from around the world!

- The GHF Customized Diet Plan, a very comprehensive nutritional program that is personally customized specifically for YOU!

- The GHF Get Motivated for Life Success System, our new motivational program.

- Fifteen FREE fitness products worth more than $500! We've developed key partnerships with other fitness-related companies to send you these at NO charge or further obligation!

3. How did the idea for Global-fitness.com come about?

In 1996 I began learning about the power and potential of the Internet and immediately began dreaming up ways of taking my personal training program to the world. I then got to work and a year later the site was launched.

4. Can you give us an idea of the size of your membership site? How many subscribers do you have, monthly revenue, number of new subscribers per week, number of employees, etc?

We have more than 35,000 members from 60 countries.

5. That's a lot of subscribers! With that many paying subscribers would your annual revenue be around 1 million or more?

Yes.

6. How long did it take for you to really start generating full-time income?

About 1 year.

7. You offer the option of the full $59.95 membership or a 30 day trial for $4.95. Do most people sign-up for your 30 day trial at $4.95? If so, what kind of percentage are you able to upgrade to full membership access?

It's about 50/50 to start and then about 45% of those that purchased the trial upgrade to full status.

8. Where do you focus most of your time and activities? Can you give us a bit of a breakdown on an average day for you?

About 14 hours a day, 5 days a week. 3-5 hours on Saturday and Sunday. About 20% answering e-mails, 30% improving site (adding membership features), 20%

maintenance (accounting, newsletters, etc.) and 30% working on new membership features or products.

9. Your site is very professional. Do you do any of the design or technical work yourself?

No, none.

10. You have a great Alexa traffic ranking (about 26,600). Where do most of your visitors come from? Search engines, pay-per-click, link exchanges, etc? List in order of importance.

- Search engines

- Affiliates

- Link and content partnerships

11. When you say you use search engines - do you mean pay-per-click?

We do not pay for pay-per-click, but instead use conventional search engines. We've used a search engine optimization specialist since 1998 who has helped us literally dominate all the major search engines for the best, most relevant diet and fitness-related keywords. For example, if you go to Google.com, AOL.com, Hotbot.com, Search.Netscape.com, or Yahoo.com and search on "fitness programs," you'll see that we're the very first listing.

12. Can you list a few keywords you focus on?

Fitness programs, lose weight, fitness instruction, workout routines.

13. How often do subscribers who sign-up for your free trial, receive follow-up emails?

When people sign-up to take our Free Fitness Analysis they receive our 1-day, 5-day, 15-day, 30-day, and 90-day follow-up messages.

14. Do you have any strategic alliances or joint ventures (including link exchanges) that bring high volume traffic?

Yes, we just signed a content/revenue share deal with Yahoo. We just sent them a proposal for working together and it went from there.

15. You have great sales copy on your site. But I noticed it's not that long. How do you feel about long copy vs short copy?

Peoples' attention span is very short on the Net, so it's very important to keep it very concise and to the point.

16. Have you done any offline advertising? If so, what kind of results did you get?

Absolutely not, and do not plan to. Consider how much less likely they are to remember your URL, type it in correctly and then take action...as opposed to just clicking a link right then, when you have their attention.

17. What does it take to turn a small online business into a highly successful site like yours? Many people struggle to get past certain revenue goals. How have you continued to have great growth? Is it a matter of increasing your advertising and providing good customer service and products - or is it more than this?

So many people have got burned on the Net, so it's very important to provide impeccable customer service and provide as much reason to fight skepticism (i.e. testimonials, etc.). You need to provide very prompt, detailed replies to all inquiries and then be sure to follow up.

18. Do you feel it's important to offer subscribers something with which they can interact?

Yes, you need to make the Internet warm and personal and offer the ability to consult easily with your staff, as well as other customers (i.e. a forum).

19. How is your retention? Is there anything that you do in particular to keep subscribers coming back and renewing or keeping their subscriptions?

Yes, always improve the site, add new membership benefits and features, provide excellent customer service and make them offers to renew. Our members renew about 55% of the time.

20. Do you offer any additional services or gifts if someone re-subscribers?

Yes, we continually make offers until they either renew or say that they absolutely do not want to. This is anything from books, to fat calipers, to additional months added when they renew, etc.

21. What kind of strategy do you use to separate yourself from your competitors?

The very best, most personalized service.

22. What kind of conversion rate do you have for your site? (Unique visitors to paying customers)

About 1 in 350.

23. What would be the most important thing you would say to someone trying to start and promote his own membership site?

Prompt customer service is key, as well as continually improving and updating the site.

* Chad has BS degrees in Exercise and Health Science and Nutrition from Oregon State University (Corvallis, OR) and is certified as a professional Personal Trainer and Weight Management Specialist. Additional professional education has included several dozen personal trainer/health-and-fitness seminars taught by professionals from around the world, including Heart Zone Training from Sally Edwards and Shaping the Future of Exercise (Drs. James Peterson and Cedric Bryant).

Part 2
Setting up your
Membership Site

CHAPTER 4

From idea to membership site, a hypothetical step-by-step scenario

The anatomy of a membership site - Watch as we turn an idea into a cash-flow producing membership site, with no experience and almost no budget. What would you do to turn your idea into a profitable membership site? Follow along as we show you how to piece it all together...

To show you what's involved in planning, creating and deploying a membership site from conception to completion, we'll follow the experience of a hypothetical company as it develops from idea to fully functional membership site.

From idea to product

There are thousands of would-be independent filmmakers in the US and around the world. The question is, do any of them search for information online, or more importantly do they buy information/products online?

Our hypothetical company will be on filmmaking. We'll call it TheFilmMakersClub.com or TFMC.com for short.

Step one: Testing the viability of an idea

Referring to Overture Search Term TFMC.com discovers that over 4,528 people search each month on one search engine alone, for information on producing independent films, specifically the keyword 'filmmaking'. Looking good. To further validate demand TFMC.com enters that keyword into Google.com, taking note of ads (Google Adwords that appear), and the top ranking sites. A number of sites offer books, videos and home study courses. Competition isn't always a bad thing - it can be a great research tool, validating demand.

A quick search on Alexa.com for a number of the sites shows a good traffic ranking, additional topics, and products purchased from Amazon.com (if any). This information is useful for possible joint ventures and to once again confirm demand for the subject. Finally TFMC.com signs-up to similar websites to receive their free bulletins, tips, etc., and studies what they are offering.

People who are interested in this site also bought:

- The Complete Guide to American Film Schools and O... by Ernest Pintoff $13.30
- Projections 12: Filmmakers on Film Schools by John Boorman $14.00
- Careers for Film Buffs & Other Hollywood Types by Jaq Greenspon $10.36
- What They Don't Teach You at Film School: 161 Stra... by Camille Landau $11.20
- Hollywood 101: The Film Industry by Frederick Levy $13.97
- Breaking & Entering: Land Your First Job in Film P... by April Fitzsimmons $12.57
- Film Directing Shot by Shot: Visualizing from Conc... by Steven D. Katz $19.57

Screen shot section of Alex.com: This is a great resource for ideas on headlines and to see what kind of products your target market is willing to spend money on. A little more research shows there are courses, books, etc. on film making, costing hundreds and even thousands of dollars. Our target market has money!

Step two: A membership site is born

The all important 'Offer'

With these ideas and research in mind, now comes the critical step of developing the 'Offer'. If TFMC.com gets this wrong, all their other efforts will be in vain.

Your offer should be all about "What's in it for the customer." What do they get for their hard earned money? Make your product seem way under priced for the value they are receiving. Offers should be kept simple. TFMC.com creates their offer...

"Subscribers will receive 24/7 access to exclusive inside information on how independent films are produced - from people who are actually doing it. Including behind-the-scenes eVideo footage of independent films in the making, how the films were financed, produced and distributed. Subscribers can access audio interviews with successful independent filmmakers. They can read articles on digital filmmaking, screen writing, production and how to get a film 'picked-up.' Finally, they'll receive 5 free sets of the eAudio course titled 'Become a World Famous Independent Filmmaker.' They also have the chance to win an 'on-the-set invitation' to an independent film in the making, where they can work side-by-side with the director for 1 week. Plus, if they are the first 300 subscribers to sign-up they will receive a discount coupon at selected film equipment stores worth $200. All for only $29.97 quarterly."

Step three: Producing the site and the package

The design and production stage

Below is the sequence of events in putting it all together...

1. TFMC.com posts a bid on eLance.com to have their logo and/or web page top banner designed.

2. Sales copy is written, including a strong headline and bullet points explaining the benefits of subscribing.

3. Once logo/banner is received, TFMC.com designs the layout of the site in their favorite html editor, or uses a template. Members' only area is also designed.

4. A form is added to the site to include a 'Free Tip of the Week/Audio interview with an independent filmmaker.'

5. A sign-up page for membership access is designed.

6. Credit card processing is integrated (paypal.com, 2checkout.com, paysystems.com, ibill.com, etc.)

7. Membership management software is installed. Available from MembershipSiteAdvisor.com

Product development

How does TFMC.com put together all of the products mentioned in their offer in the shortest possible time? Here's a list and a description of how they put the package together in record time. All of these bonuses will only be available to active subscribers.

1. Behind the scenes eVideo footage: They contact independent film makers, even if they've already completed production and ask them for their 'media pack' and any behind the scenes footage. Filmmakers are more than willing to supply this information. It's promotion for their film. They'll love TFMC.com for it. TFMC.com finds a list of independent films in the making by going to: http://indie.imdb.com/index.indie

2. Audio Interviews: When contacting the independent filmmakers, TFMC.com invites them to be phone interviewed. The phone interview is recorded (with permission of course) and turned into an MP3 file.

3. Articles: Email colleges and publishers that specialize in filmmaking. TFMC.com easily finds them on search engines, yellow pages, etc. Once contact has been made, they are emailed or phoned with a list of questions. The answers can then be used as either a case study or an article.

4. Five Set eAudio course: 'Become a World Famous Independent Film Maker', is produced by phone interviewing a small, but known independent filmmaker (known in their industry, not necessarily to the public). This person can be contacted through their agent or their website. TFMC.com just searches their name on a search engine. How does TFMC.com know who is famous in their industry? Well, they should probably already know because this is their passion - however they can know right away by browsing some trade magazines, online articles and ezines.

5. Win an 'on-the-set invitation': Once again, after contacting independent film producers, TFMC.com explains the competition and the promotion their film will receive and gets permission to have one of their subscribers come on the set.

6. Discount coupon: TFMC.com contacts a chain of film equipment stores and asks them what discount offer they can give to our subscribers to bring them into the stores. Store owners will love the promotion TFMC.com is going to give them. TFMC.com also talks about the possibility of a Joint Venture, where the store can give out TFMC.com coupons to their customers for a 6 month free subscription to TFMC.com's Members area. The store is happy to return the favor, and add value to their customer services.

The entire package and members area are now completed!

Step four: Test marketing - the start of cash flow

TFMC.com tests their new site using Google Adwords, setting about 10 related keywords at 5 cents a click.
Average conversion is 1.5% from traffic generated.
Minor adjustments in copy and new guarantee that states, "You'll learn how to make your own movie in 6 months or we'll refund you in full" takes conversion up to 2.5% - 3%.

The breakdown stats are:

100 clicks @ 5 cents each: $5
2 new subscribers per 100 clicks @ 2% conversion: $59.94 gross profit

* Over 10 times the ROI (Return on Investment)

Results are good.

TFMC.com gets ready for the full roll-out.

Step five: Full marketing roll-out: TFMC.com's founder quits his day job!

- Set up joint ventures with similar sites and relevant target market sites - Including link exchanges, ad swaps in ezines, and affiliate programs.

- Increase Google Adwords budget

- Increase the number of keywords used.

- Advertise on other search engines (tracking results): Overture.com, FindWhat.com, Kanoodle.com, GoClick.com, etc.

- Run ads in ezines (search enzines by going to ezine-universe.com. TFMC.com also contacts the ezines signed up to previsouly)

- Magazines and online newsletters contacted with offers for 6 month free subscription to their subscribers

- Press releases to magazines, and online newsletters.

- Set up affiliate program offering ongoing 30% commission to affiliates.

The president of TFMC.com quits his telemarketing job that he loves so much, and becomes a full time membership publisher!

CHAPTER 5

Website design strategies that boost subscriptions

Is your web design killing your sales? Do you know which colors to use, which fonts work the best, where to place graphics, etc?

Which is more important, web copy or web design? The answer is web copy - kind of. What many don't realize, is that if your design looks amateurish or confuses a visitor, your web copy may not even get read.

You see, it's becoming more and more important to impress someone as soon as they hit your site. But more importantly, people DON'T read websites - they SCAN them (at least to start with). If you don't have your web design ready to handle the "scanner," you're probably missing out on new subscriptions.

Rule #1: Design for the 'Scanners' - and we're all 'Scanners'

As mentioned, visitors scan web pages. So how does this affect your web design and your web copy?

People want information fast. When we visit a site, we want to know as soon as possible if it has 'the goods.' If not, you'll hit the back button and search for another site. So in the process of making this decision, you're searching headlines, subheads, demos, links, graphics, etc.

You may want your website to be read from top to bottom, like the example below. But...

...more than likely it will be read something like this...

How we think and process a site

Below is the basic process we go through when visiting a site. Below each topic is what we need to do to answer the questions. And we'd better answer those questions fast, or our visitor will say "NEXT."

Do you read the entire newspaper? More than likely, you will quickly scan each page and read only the articles that jump out. We're in information overload - but we want more. However, to do this we have to 'sort' and only read what we want and discard the rest.

It's important to note, that how someone finds your site will change the process. For example, if someone is searching for the exact product you offer, they might skip 1, 2, 3 and go straight to "is it better than xyz product?"

1. What's it all about?

Headline should immediately answer this question.

2. Is this what I'm looking for?

Headline and first paragraph should answer this question and create strong curiosity to keep reading.

3. What's in it for me?

Headline

4. Is it better than xyz product?

USP (unique selling proposition - what's different about your product), product demo, documented 3rd party certification, awards, white papers, case studies, etc.

5. Can I trust this company?

Testimonials, case studies, free trials, risk free trial, documented 3rd party info, respected (celebrity or professional) endorsements.

Will visitors read your entire site?

Some will, some won't. That's not important. What is important is that you give them enough information to make a decision, and that they can make that decision whenever they want - without having to work out how to make it!

Your goal is to instantly 'hook' a visitor (using effective copy and layout) and keep teasing them with more and more information until they have enough to make a decision.

To do this effectively means having a sign-up or purchase button near the top of every page. It also requires headlines and bullet points peppered throughout your page - to catch the scanner's eye. You never know which hot button will do the trick.

As though your visitors have a small scale inside their head, they are weighing up whether or not your site is worth their time. The more hot buttons you hit, the more subscribers you'll get.

Positioning sign-up buttons on your web page

Allowing visitors to make a decision when they want isn't too difficult. Firstly, make sure that there are sign-up buttons at the top of every page. So at any point a visitor can sign-up or purchase.

We always place a 'join now' link near the top of every page....

Audible.com (a highly successful membership site) does this well also...

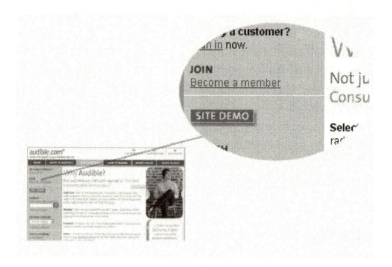

Rule #2: The most important question to answer on your site

What is this site offering... what is it all about?

The instant your target market arrives at your site and reads your opening line, they should know instantly what it's all about. You'll notice I used the words "your target market". Your web copy doesn't have to make sense to anyone except your target market. But it needs to immediately make sense to your target market. Don't make them guess. They won't. They'll leave.

Rule #3: The second most important question to answer on your site

What's in it for me?

This is only the second most important because you have to know the first before you can answer it. Ideally both questions should be incorporated and answered together.

The only way you can let a visitor know "what's in it for me", is to have an effective headline.

Rule #4: Are your web graphics hurting your sales?

Poorly designed graphics can hurt your credibility and also turn away a visitor before you have a chance to 'hook' them.

If you're designing your own top banner graphics, try to incorporate an object photo (a photo without a background. Sometimes called 'isolated' photos). This will give your site a professional feel.

As far as positioning, there are no set rules. However, try to avoid using too many graphics on a page. Not only does this clutter your site, but it also slows the download speed.

It's important to also show an image of your product, whether it's digital or physical. Photos of your product, along with captions can really boost sales. For example, one of our software packages is only a digital product, but we still had a box graphics designed for it. Under the box is a small description and details on getting it for free.

Low cost and free photo stock

Using professional graphics needn't be expensive. Try the following resource:

www.sxc.hu - Offers 50,000 quality stock photos, supplied by "photography addicts who generously offer their works to the public free of charge."

www.iStockPhoto.com - has a great library of graphics, at very low cost (0.50 cents - to $1.50 a photo). They also offer a lot of object photos, which is the preferred format for Web designers. A great way to add that professional touch to your site.

Rule #5: Choosing the right Web colors

One of the first things I learnt while studying advertising in California was that you should never use more than 3 colors when designing promotional material. The Net is the same. Unless you're a design expert don't use any more than 3 colors on your site.

Pick colors that conform. For example, the "bumble bee colors" - yellow and black.

Also pick colors that create positive emotions. For example, you'll notice that many sites use navy blue. Navy blue gives visitors a warm feeling. It's said to create trust.

Rule #6: Choosing the best fonts

Stick to standard fonts. We like to use Arial (point size 10) for our body copy.

Like colors, you shouldn't use any more than 3 different font styles.

Rule #7: The 8 second download rule

ZDNet.com reported that any web pages that took longer than 8 seconds to download at 56K—cost businesses $362 million collectively, in 2000

It's important you optimize your site and graphics to download quickly. This means not having too many graphics on your page, and making sure they are resized correctly.

A final tip:

Whether your site is due for a makeover or you're just getting started, one of the best things you can do is to study other websites. Make sure you're studying those that successfully sell a product or service. Good indicators of a successful site include:

- A high traffic ranking.

- Paid advertisements. Online and offline.

- Reports and other articles about the site.

- Press releases.

- One of the best sites to study is Amazon.com.

- Completely automate your Membership Site with a management software package.

CHAPTER 6

Membership site management software review

We feature one of the best membership site management packages on the market. Loads of features, including multiple payment systems simultaneously, multiple levels of access, and much more.

Every now and then, a great software package comes along that just does everything for you.

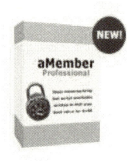

We were so impressed with the features of aMember Pro that we've decided to move our entire system over to it.

Offer multiple payment systems simultaneously

To maximize new member subscriptions, you should offer various payment methods - Credit card, PayPal, eCheck, etc.

We've had great success using only PayPal - But, we've also lost business by not offering another alternative. We now offer credit card purchasing in addition to PayPal.

Potential subscribers want options. Some prefer to pay using PayPal, others can't or don't want to use it. This software allows your subscriber to choose which option they want during the sign-up process.

Subscribers have the option of choosing their own user name. Just another thing to optimize the purchasing experience.

Do you want to offer different levels of membership?

One of my other membership sites is about to release an advanced membership level, where paying subscribers have the option to upgrade their current basic level account. Offering advanced membership is a great way to "up-sell" current subscribers. Without an application like aMember Pro, this could be a complex and time consuming activity.

aMember allows members of your site to login and update their personal payment details. For example, a member can upgrade to an advanced subscription, or renew an expired subscription. Not only is this a good management tool, it's good marketing. A lot of expired subscriptions can be recovered if a simple system is in place for them to renew. aMember Pro will allow an expired member to login using their old password and re-subscribe.

Using aMember Pro 'Coupon' tool as a Joint Venture deal maker

We've recently put together a joint venture deal where, to create a win win situation, we needed to offer a 3 month membership to our site for free. Basically the deal goes like this - whenever a customer purchases our joint venture partner's product, the customer also receives a coupon that allows them to have 3 months access to our site, after which time this expires or their credit card is charged to continue the subscription. Here's a breakdown of the deal.

1. Our joint venture partner has a non-competitive product that has a similar target market to ours.

2. To create an ideal win/win/win situation for all involved, we had to offer a free subscription. Why? Because we wanted our joint venture partner to offer a 3 month subscription to our site as a premium or gift to all of his customers. This made it easy for us to set-up the deal.

3. Everyone wins. The joint venture partner wins because he has now added a power premium to his product (our membership site) at no cost whatsoever to him. The customer wins, because they get a free subscription to our site. We win because a high percentage of the free trial users will stay on to become paying subscribers, after the 3 months.

Now, if you didn't have a system in place to handle this kind of deal, it could get complicated and messy, especially when you have several joint ventures all going at once. Imagine trying to track which joint venture deals were the most profitable, handling the expiration of members after the 3 months, setting up a special page that offers customers the 3 month subscription, etc. Sounds hard! But there's an easy way....

aMember allows you to create a coupon number (with a few clicks) to a subscription product. So that means, all you have to do is create a coupon number for your different joint venture partners and presto... all of the above is taken care of automatically. All the tracking, all the free sign-ups, all the expiring and all the new payments at the end of the free trial term. There's nothing to do but generate your coupon number - which takes 60 seconds, if that.

All the customer has to do is enter the coupon number at time of sign-up.

The dialogue we use to set up these kinds of joint ventures

On first contacting a potential joint venture partner, our dialogue usually goes something like this...

```
"Hi Bob,

We came across your product (name the
product) while searching for (the keyword)
on Google.

Our customers would be very interested to
hear about your (name the product). Would
you be interested in doing a joint venture
between our companies where we could both
mail out information to our lists? We would
be happy to offer your customers and any new
customers a free subscription to our site,
thereby adding a lot of value to your
current product at no cost to you.

I welcome any ideas you might have.

Looking forward to hearing back from you

Warmly,
```

As I've said many times, one good joint venture can set you up. One of our joint ventures over the Christmas break brought in over 1,500 new ezine subscribers to our "tip of the week" in less than 2 weeks and a good percentage converted into paying customers. The usual slow month of Christmas turned out to be our highest netting month ever.

Here are some of the major functions of aMember Pro:

- Integrated with multiple payment systems. Able to support multiple payment systems simultaneously.

- Special cookie login interface, where members can login, review payments and renew subscription. Your visitors will never see the ugly browser log-in window again!

- Support for multiple products with different prices, period of subscription and level of access.

- Can be used as stand-alone user management script.

- Easily add/modify/remove members.

- Automated signups and mail to new and expired users.

- Manage an unlimited number of members.

- Can be used to setup free areas on site, requiring only registration, not payment (possible after admin approval).

- Easy web based administration, all management is done through your browser.

- aMember doesn't force you to change your website. It will stay in a separate folder, providing payment and member login functions. Any other folders on your site may be set to "members-only" access mode.

- Easily change the complete look and feel of the software, including login screens.

- Payment system support is based on plug-ins, so new payment gateways can be easily added.

- Protection plug-ins: The script handles authorization using plug-ins. Additional plug-ins can be easily added to provide integration with customer support software, forums, etc.

- aMember is a PHP/MySQL based script, works faster and is easier to customize than Perl.

- Requirements: Your server will need these before aMember will run (most servers have the following).

    - PHP 4.0.6 or later version.

    - MySQL 3.22 or later version.

    - Unix/Linux hosting.

For more information on aMember and to download a trial version go to:
www.MembershipSiteAdvisor.com/amember

CHAPTER 7

Getting exclusive content from experts & speaking with famous people

You'd be surprised what contacts you can make when you own a membership site. We've interviewed millionaires to world champion athletes. Here's how we do it!

Networking with the Experts

There's one word that will change the way you approach experts and famous people from now on – "interview." If you want to increase your knowledge, credibility, and gain valuable exclusive content, then you need to interview the experts. Fortunately it's not hard when the approach is right.

You can interview people you thought were untouchable – heroes in your eyes. Someone you thought you would only read about, or whose work you'd study. That's exciting! That's powerful! A membership site gives you the excuse to learn from amazing people... how can this not help you succeed in life?

Just this week we set up an interview with a well known public speaker. He's received awards from President George Bush, has been featured on National TV in over 100 countries, and made millions of dollars in his industry. So how did we get a personal interview with this guy? Simple, we contacted him and asked for an "exclusive interview."

The thing is, experts and famous people want the exposure. Not only that, but it gives them a chance to share their story. When you approach them with an interview offer... most are thrilled and honored at the thought. Even better, you're the one who's usually in control. Often they will chase you - a good position to be in.

Conducting interviews will allow you to enter the "inner circle." All experts have their contacts - a select few associates! When you interview the expert and build that relationship, it will most likely lead you to other joint ventures and networks. It's a never-ending source of business and information. Membership sites lead themselves to this style of exclusive marketing.

5 Steps to Getting an Exclusive Interview

1. Work hard on getting your first interview with an expert. Once you've got one, the rest is all downhill. Interviewing an expert also gives you instant credibility and a network of other experts! 6 degrees of separation. It's like mining for gold.
2. Have a professional, credible site. Experts have a reputation to protect. If they feel your site will damage their reputation or lower their credibility, they won't talk to you.
3. Contact them by email and phone. Try to get a response from your email first and then follow up with a phone call to strengthen the relationship and

run through some interview ideas. In some cases you may have to use snail mail or fax. If you make the initial contact by phone, don't assume it's a good time to talk. Set up a time. That's your goal.

4. Establish yourself as a credible source of good information. How? By researching and writing, recording or producing quality content or tools.

5. Learn to write. Contact less well known experts and work your way up. Exclusive Interviews means more Traffic and Customers.

Having experts on your site can create a tidal wave of viral traffic for your business. You see, you've now got something completely unique from a trusted source and you're the only one who has it. People will eagerly pass this kind of exclusive content onto others.

The very nature of this concept is viral. People love news, stories and gossip. You can give them all 3.

Who's an Expert? Where should you start?

- Government personnel
- Periodical staff writers
- Convention speakers
- Company personnel
- University professors
- Book authors
- Editors
- Consultants
- Professional associations
- People with hands-on experience
- Athletes

Where to find them?

Check out the bookstores, libraries, magazines, Yellow Pages, Internet. Where do you go to find information on your topic? Whose books have you purchased? What articles do you read? Which magazines do you buy? They are easy to find and easy to contact.

Who knows, you might even set up a joint venture with them...

In most cases you will both have a common customer.

Real-Life Case Study #3

Virtual Cooking school signs-up hundreds of paying subscribers

Video tutorial, articles, snap shots and bulletin boards are what this membership site is all about. As featured in the New York Times, this French cook

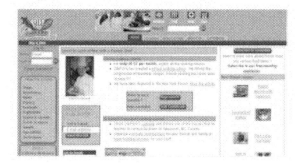

now has hundreds of monthly paying subscribers/ students. He shares some of his technical and marketing tips and tricks.

1. Hi Eric, can you tell us a little bit about your background?

Sure. I'm originally from France, but I studied in Canada to teach French cooking, and now live in Canada.

2. How did you come up with the idea for 911ChefEric.com

Well, during my studies in Canada, one of my assignments was to come up with a website. So I did. Upon presenting the assignment, my teacher at the time said I had to put a title or name to it. I hadn't really thought about a name, so as a joke I asked my students (I was also teaching while studying) to come up with a domain name. My students came up with the name chef911.com. I was surprised by the name. As it turns out my students had previously nicknamed me "chef 911," because I'm always helping students with their cooking problems.

I still just saw the site as a college assignment. However my wife was saying how I put all this time into it and that I should go ahead and promote it. Thus chef911 became a business.

3. Did you design the site yourself?

No, I contracted someone to design and build the backend of the site.

I only do the recipes and produce the videos that are shown in the members' area.

4. So you video yourself?

Yes. I set up a tripod and use a remote control to start the video camera recording.

5. What kind of camera do you use? Is it digital?

I use a Cannon digital camera to produce my videos.

I also edit the clips myself. Originally it took me a long time to produce each one. Now that I have more experience, I'm able to spend a lot less time putting together the videos.

All of the editing is done on my PC. I also use Photoshop to create graphics for each clip.

6. How many videos are in your members' area? What software do you use to compress and stream the video for the web?

About 320. Each clip lasts anywhere between 30 seconds to 4 minutes. Longer clips are broken up into slide shows.

I use up about 1 Gig of memory on my server.

All of my videos are compiled into QuickTime format.

In the future, I plan on turning the videos into cooking DVDs as additional promotional and backend products.

7. Can you give us an idea of the size of your membership site? How many paying subscribers do you have?

Most of my subscribers are based in the US, followed by Canada.

We currently have several hundred subscribers. All on recurring billing.

8. Do you employ anyone to help you run the site?

No, I run the business myself. I do all the marketing, the video production, the updating etc. I do contract out work that I can't do, or don't have time to do, like website design.

Currently I run the business part-time, and the other half of my time is taken up teaching in actual person.

9. Is that where most of your subscribers come from? Do they come from your seminars, classes, etc?

No. About 20% come from classes and seminars. The other 80% I have never met. They find my site directly online or through some other promotion.

10. When did you launch your membership site?

November, 2002.

11. You mentioned that 80% of your subscribers come from online marketing. What is your main form of online marketing?

I promote my site on the major search engines.

- Google

- Overture

- Altavista

But the only one that really works for me is Google Adwords. I still have an account with Overture, but the actual clicks are a bit slow, I still have over 80% of my budget left on Overture.

I've found that keywords that work well on Google don't necessarily work very well on Overture.

5. Earn Your Online Degree
A guide to online colleges and online universities. Earn your degree entirely online. Hundreds of programs available. Request more information today.
www.earnyouronlinedegree.com (sponsored listing)

6. Online College Degrees
College degrees available from accredited online colleges and universities. Earn your Associate's, Bachelor's, Master's and Doctorate degrees online. Request more information today.
www.onlineschools4you.com (sponsored listing)

7. Online Cooking Classes ⟵
Get your own French Chef Instructor with pre-recorded on line cooking classes, to guide you step-by-step. It shows you how easy it is to create a French style meals and amaze your friends.
www.911cheferic.com (sponsored listing)

8. Culinary Business Academy
Culinary Business Academy. World class training for first class success. Train to be a personal chef, caterer or train to work in a commercial kitchen.
www.culinarybusiness.com (sponsored listing)

12. Have you tried any other forms of marketing?

Yes. I've run ads in some magazines, newspapers and some trade journals.

13. How was the response to this offline advertising?

Not good. I've found that offline advertising doesn't seem to work too well when you're just promoting a website.

14. We've found the same thing. We've run some magazine ads and they just didn't pull in the responses. Now, you were also featured in the New York Times. Was that something where they found out about you, or did you submit a press release?

No, they just found my site and phoned me. They asked if they could interview me about the site. I said sure, when?

They said "how about right now?". So they interviewed me and released the article in July.

15. Did you get a good response from the New York Times?

Actually we did. Our traffic went up about 600% when the article came out.

16. For your online promotions, how do you go about choosing your keywords?

I just target people looking for "online cooking classes", "French cooking", "learn to cook." I only run about 100 keywords.

Out of the 100 keywords, I only get about 25% that really pull in traffic.

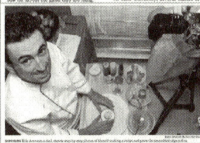

THE NEW YORK TIMES, THURSDAY, OCTOBER 16, 2003

Can't Even Boil Water?
Your Mouse Can Help

By BONNIE ROTHMAN MORRIS

** *AUTHOR'S NOTE:* Yes, we've found the same. About 20% of our keywords pull in 80% of our traffic. We find the keywords using 'keyword suggestion tools'. Another little trick once you find a keyword that pulls really well, is to then run a keyword suggestion on that word. It will give you a whole new range of keywords. Out of that list you will have a few winners. We take the winners and repeat the process. We keep doing this until we have at least 1000 keywords.

17. On another topic - do you feel that it's important to have something with which your subscribers can interact?

It's essential. Also fresh content is needed. We make sure that we have new content every week. We not only update the members' area each week, but we also update the home page.

I find that visitors or potential subscribers return to check out what's new. I also give away some free things like recipes. But to watch any of the videos, you have to be a paying subscriber.

18. How long does it normally take you to do a video clip?

It normally takes me about 7 hours to do a 2 minute clip. That includes creating the recipes, shopping for the ingredients, shooting the video, and editing it. It sometimes takes me 2 days to get it finished and uploaded to the members' area.

19. And what's your subscriber retention like?

I have a few that just sign up for one month or 3 months. But most sign up and stay with us. We only have about a 2% cancellation rate.

20. Wow, that's great retention. Do you have many competitors or are you fairly unique?

We have a few competitors, but they are a little different to us. So we are fairly unique.

21. What kind of software do you use to manage your membership site?

I had the entire backend of my membership site just built. It's all web-based, running from our server. I was recently in France (for Christmas) and was able to run my entire business while I was overseas. It's really great to have that kind of freedom, to run it from anywhere in the world.

22. And you use WorldPay.com to process credit cards, and manage your recurring billing? How have you found them?

They are awesome! We've had great service from them. They are very efficient.

23. How many subscribers do you have for your free newsletter (ezine)?

We have just over 2,000 subscribers.

24. Is your newsletter an HTML newsletter?

Yes. It includes photos of the recipes, etc.

25. What do you plan to do to increase or expand your business and the number of subscribers you have?

The site continues to grow each month. We are getting more and more subscribers. I plan on doing some of the following things to increase the business...

I will increase my Google Adwords. I feed about 25% of my profits back into marketing. My overheads are really low, so I can afford to put a fair amount into advertising.

We also plan to improve the site.

One of our big plans is to open an actual shop. We will tie the website into the shop and make it a part of the promotions.

We will probably also release a DVD set of my lessons. This will be sold on our site, and promoted from our newsletter.

Sounds like you are building a great little business. Thank you for your time today Eric. We wish you all the best with your membership site.

Part 3
How to promote your Membership Site to the world

CHAPTER 8

Part 1: Using the eBay/Google partnership to win new subscribers at very low cost

"When someone is looking to buy a product, you can be sure they have visited one or both of these two sites..."

Have you ever sold anything on eBay? Here's how to use eBay to auction off subscriptions to your membership site or selected content from your site.

Have you ever noticed that when you search for a product on Google, up pops a Google ad for eBay? Why? Because eBay has a special deal with Google that allows their ads to show up when certain keywords are searched.

That means you can have 2 of the highest hit websites both co-promoting your membership site, but only if you are also selling your products and membership site on eBay. eBay is paying for the Google ad - of course you have to share the spotlight with other listings, but the visitor will be a highly targeted buyer. They are there to buy!

How to list your Membership Site on eBay

You basically have two choices when it comes to getting new subscribers via eBay:

1. Auctioning off a subscription

- Basically with this approach, eBay becomes your landing page (sales page). Your goal is to provide your sales pitch on your eBay page and then make reference and links to your membership site. You may even want to try to encourage eBay visitors to sign-up to your ezine to test it out!

It's also a good idea to link to some articles about your membership site. We normally provide links on articles that have been published by a 3rd party - such as PrWeb (a press release announcement service – see www.PrWeb.com) and magazines. You might even consider audio files, like a radio interview.

- Once the bid has been won, simply issue the winner a discount coupon (if using aMember). On the following recurring bill, it will automatically return to the normal price. Make sure that all bidders understand this.

2. Auction off physical products

- Your second option is to turn some of your content into a book, report, or CD (even a DVD if you have video files) and auction them off as separate products.

- The fastest way to create a physical product to sell on eBay is to turn some of your articles into a report or actual book. In fact, we are having that done right now.

- You can also have any audio file or interview transcribed and sell them off as a book.. In fact a fast way to create an entire book is to pay someone to transcribe audio interviews conducted by you. We used RentaCoder.com to contract someone to do this for us. It's very inexpensive - you'd be surprised how much work you can save yourself at very little cost.

- Alternatively just turn your audio files into a CD course and sell it on eBay. Even throw in a book to sweeten the deal.

So would you choose to auction off a subscription or to sell a physical product?

My pick is to create the physical products and a combination of CDs, a Book and even a DVD. This will sell on eBay as a course. This course will then encourage customers to continue their eduction by signing up to MSA. My strategy is to use the physical products as a lead generator for my membership site.

There's one more advantage to auctioning off a physical product. eBay buyers love to see real-life photos of the product being sold. Although a screen shot of your members' area will work well, you may find a photo of an actual product will do better - depending on your target market of course.

eBay and Google

I don't have to tell you that two of the biggest names on the Internet are eBay and Google. When someone is looking to buy a product, you can be sure they have visited one or both of these two sites.

What many people tend to overlook is that you can instantly have your products listed on both sites. And eBay has a special deal with Google where certain keyword searches will show up on Google's adwords. So eBay even promotes your product category for you. Will this increase your traffic? You bet!

How to sell on eBay

Because eBay is so inexpensive to advertise on, you have the opportunity to test pricing, sales copy, and get immediate exposure. Below are some tips you should follow when selling on eBay.

- Do your eBay research: Research the market value of similar products. Before you list a particular product on eBay, spend some time using the advanced search feature to generate a list of "completed items" and their end price. What was the final price? If you set your minimum bid or reserve too high, no one will bid. If you set it too low, you kill your profits. Simply follow the bidding process. Statistically you will be able to gauge the interest in your product and determine a price or no price!

- Try testing different prices: For example, instead of auctioning off a one month subscription, try offering a one year subscription. Even if the one year membership is heavily discounted, you may find the upfront fee more appealing than just a one month subscription. You will also have the potential of converting bidders who didn't win, but signed up to your ezine.

- Always Include a Photo: A picture is worth a thousand words. There is a very small percentage of items that don't require a photograph. Provide multiple photographs for high end products.

- Word your auction Title carefully: Your auction title should include keywords that buyers are likely to use when searching for your item. Look for hot buttons that will attract bidders, but make the title clear.

- Write your eBay listing like you would a great ad: Put as much information (avoid hype) about the item as you can. As mentioned, include links, statistics, examples, testimonials, stories, etc. Lack of information will reduce the number of bids - meaning a lower sell price. Be sure to include keyword phrases, hot keyword phrases. These will be picked up by the search engines.

- Be business-like: Answer inquiries immediately to gain the trust of bidders.

- Offer multiple payment options, including credit cards: The more payment options you can offer, the more bids you'll receive for your membership site or products. Give as many options as possible.

- Your reputation is important: If you've ever bought on eBay, what's one of the first things you do after you find a product at the right price? You check the seller's feedback. If he doesn't score well, you might not trust him with your money. On eBay, many non-business people sell their personal items, so people tend to rely heavily on feedback ratings. Make sure yours ranks high.

Getting your site listed on two of the highest hit websites will certainly increase your traffic. And auctioning off memberships is just the beginning. Many will sign-up to your free ezine and later convert into full paying subscribers. All this for a few dollars spent on an eBay listing. What have you got to lose?

CHAPTER 9

Part 2: Using the eBay/Google partnership to win new subscribers at very low cost

"... the second listing had an ROI of almost 40 times the cost of the ad! I like those results! What kind of results could you get using these same principles?"

How we used eBay to bring in highly qualified traffic from only 3 cents a click, and a return on advertising dollars of more than 35 times the ad cost. Actual screen shots included.

Imagine a place were you can get highly qualified buyers to your site for only 3 cents a click. Well, that place is eBay.

It's all about the Keywords

Once again keywords rule. The same ad, 2 different tests changing only the keywords in the title, and dramatically different results.

Selecting the right keywords meant much higher bids and a lot more direct traffic to our site. So how do you pick the right keyword?

Keyword selection rules we follow

Select keywords where listed items are receiving a lot of bids. One of the best ways to accomplish this is to type in keywords you feel target your market. Then check if the items listed are getting bids.

The bidders in your chosen category must have money.

You can identify this by looking at other products in the same category within which you want to list your ad. For example, some of the products in the same keyword category as my listing were selling for hundreds of dollars. So I know this target market in general is willing to pay for value if they find it. I want to avoid groups of people not willing to go above 5 or 10 dollars.

Study the keywords you type in when searching for things to buy on eBay. If you are passionate about the topic of your membership site, you probably search for products on eBay for products that aren't entirely related, but may still be the same target market. We used this successfully to choose a keyword that wasn't exactly related to our topic, but we knew that if these same people saw our listing we would have a winner. And it worked.

For example, let's say you are interested in home theater projectors – a similar market might be people searching for "Plasma TVs."

Understand that keywords that work on Google may not work as well on eBay.

Our hottest pulling Google keyword didn't fair the best on eBay and vice versa. Our hottest keyword on eBay didn't pull much at all on Google. You'll need to test and modify your listings to find the best ones. However, starting with hot keywords on Google or Overture is a good place to begin.

Test results

Details of Listings
(exact same ad used in both cases)

Listing #1 - Poor keyword choice

Starting bid: $1
Listing cost: $1.20
Length of bid: 5 days
ROI: about 12 times
Cost per hit: 10 cents per visitor

Listing #2 - Good keyword choice

Starting bid: $1
Listing cost: $1.20
Length of bid: 5 days
ROI: Almost 40 times
* Cost per hit: around 3.5 cents per visitor
* *To keep things simple, we did not include the small sales commission eBay charges.*

As you can see, the second listing had an ROI of almost 40 times the cost of the ad! I like those results! What kind of results could you get using these same principles?

All we did is locate the right keywords. Spend your time searching for the best keywords.

It can make the difference between a 12 times ROI or a 40 times ROI. Which would you prefer for the same effort?

eBay V's Google

Who do you think gave the better ROI (return on investment) and cost per click? We were surprised to find that initial results favored eBay. eBay's tests averaged 22 times ROI, whereas similar tests on Google averaged 10 times ROI.

Of course this doesn't mean eBay is a better marketing tool, as the traffic and sales from Google certainly came in at larger volumes, even though the return on advertising dollar was not as high.

Both are great traffic and sales generators!

*Please note that results would vary over a longer test period

If you want a simple, fast and low risk way to start generating sales, this has got to be one of the best.

Advantages and disadvantages of auctioning subscriptions

As I mentioned in part one, you basically have 2 choices when it comes to promoting your membership site on eBay. You can choose to auction off a subscription or you can sell a tangible product, like a book or CD and those products can then lead back to your site.

Due to delays with our printed book, we didn't have the chance to auction off a tangible product. However we plan to do this with the release of this book.

There are advantages and disadvantages to the 2 options:

Auctioning a subscription - Advantages

- You can't really suffer a loss even if you start the bidding at $1, as there are no production or printing costs to cover.

- You don't have to set up fulfillment as you would for a physical product.

- No shipping costs for the buyer.

- No waiting for the buyer to receive the product.

- You can back-end physical products like CDs, DVDs, books, etc at a later date at the full retail price.

- A membership usually has a higher perceived value than a book.

Auctioning a subscription - Disadvantages

- Your winning bidder isn't on automatic recurring billing, as he's made a single purchase. You can follow-up with him when his subscription expires, but this won't be as easy if he's already on recurring billing in the first place.

- To keep the bidding price high, you may have to add some additional bonuses, as eBay buyers are looking for good deals. Although I have to admit that the ending bid can still go very high if the membership site or product is popular.

- A membership site usually won't have as high a perceived value as a DVD or CD course.

Auctioning a Book, CD, DVD, etc - Advantages

- The book can become the lead generator for the membership site. This allows you to sell subscriptions as a back-end product - a very powerful technique, as you've already established credibility as a published author.

- A DVD or CD course can really be a huge advantage. Not only does it have the same advantages as a book, but it can sell for hundreds of dollars on eBay.

Auctioning a Book, CD, DVD, etc - Disadvantages

- You have to set up distribution.

- You have to set up printing and possible inventory (unless using a print-on-demand company).

- You have printing costs, which means if you start the bid at $1 and the winning bidder gets it for $5, and it costs you $8 to print the book - well, then you just had an ROI of minus $3. Of course this can be avoided by starting the bid at the breakeven price of the book's production costs.

- You will need to charge shipping and handling. Although this usually isn't an issue.

What if?

Let's take this to the next level. The part I get excited about, is what if I run 20 listings (they only cost $1.20 each) or even 100 listings, under multiple categories? How much will I increase my traffic and number of subscribers?

Start doing your keyword research and just run your eBay ad. It's only a $1.20. How many times can you fail or test before you get it right at that price? I would think a lot of times! I remember when I used to run newspaper ads and each would cost at least $2,000. We HAD to get it right first time, every time. Now if that didn't work, well, we just wouldn't eat for a month. But at a $1.20 per eBay listing, the worst case scenario is you might have to skip that can of soda. Who cares if it doesn't work well the first few times? Give it a shot, even if you think you're not ready yet.

CHAPTER 10

Getting high traffic sites to link to your membership site - even if they say "No"

"...'Bare link' exchanges rarely work - content or service based links are the new way to generate traffic from another site..."

Why do most website owners say "no" to a link exchange, but "yes" to a 'content based link?' Exchanging links can be a key source of quality traffic to your site and boost your search engine rankings, yet most web business owners go about getting them the wrong way.

Getting high traffic sites and websites with good page ranks to link to your membership site can be a challenge. In fact, many linking strategies fail. Why, because asking to "exchange" bare links (just a link and no information) doesn't work very well. Unfortunately the majority take this approach.

I consistently receive offers to link to other sites - even from website owners who have already listed me on their resource page. But I usually still avoid putting their link on my site. Apart from the reason that they may have a lower page rank, which will affect mine, I usually reject their offer, because it's not of much benefit. A link that is buried or cluttered with hundreds of other links won't bring much traffic, if any. And this is why it's hard to just exchange "bare links."

If people never see these links, they might as well not be there. It's not worth your time. There's a big difference between randomly getting as many sites to link to your website as possible and getting a small number of quality links to your site, that drive targeted traffic.

In a minute I'll share with you how we have approached high traffic sites, some who may have initially told us "no" to a link exchange, and how we got them saying "yes!" - with one simple email (exact email included below).

Finding a medium to insert your link:

Just offering a link isn't good enough. You need to offer 'embedded' links or content based links. What do I mean by embedded? Your link has to be based on content.

Let's switch this around for the moment and look at the potential customer or the visitor to a site. They are not looking for hundreds of different links to click on, they are looking for content or services, something to read, watch, use, download. Any good website owner will know this, they know they can't just list links, they need to offer content or a service/tool that contains embedded links.

Which medium works well?

Below are some ideas you can use to get your high traffic sites to link to you. Not only link to you, but to become excited about offering this information to their valuable visitors.

- Articles

- ebooks

- case studies

- audio files

- video files

- web tools

- downloadable software

Offering links as part of content or service.

As mentioned, bare link exchanges don't work - content or service based links are the most effective way to generate traffic from another site. When a website owner can see you are providing something his visitors want and it in turn positions his website as a valuable resource, you'll have a link exchange deal in the making.

How we set up link exchanges/content exchanges

We look at link exchanges as something different. In fact, I prefer to call them content exchanges, as strict link exchanges don't work too well. Start to focus on giving out information or resources rather than getting the actual link.

But you can be exchanging more than just written content. We've exchanged audio files, software, articles, etc. all that link back to us.

The exact letter we use that has almost a 90% success rate

I constantly receive link exchange emails, which go into great detail as to the advantages of linking with them. You can spot these templates a mile away and they no longer work (if they ever did)! Short, very personal emails work the best. Below is the exact letter we use, with great success.

Getting others to link to you - even if they say "no"

Using the email above or slight variations to it, we successfully had website owners agree to link to us even when they initially refused our first offer.

The above letter not only appeals to website owners from the point of view as additional traffic for them, but also that they can offer a valuable resource (like a case study) to their own visitors.

Position, position, position

As I mentioned in the beginning, if your bare link is positioned with hundreds of other bare links, it's likely you won't get any traffic at all.

But embed that link into something of value, well, that's a totally different story... Not only that, but everyone will appreciate it more. The website owner can offer quality content or services to his customers and visitors, so he's comfortable doing it. The visitor is happy to find and explore something he is interested in. You're happy because instead of getting a bare link, or a classified link (basically your URL with a 2 line description), you get a full page or several pages to plead your case and entice your reader. It's like the difference between getting an article in a leading newspaper or running a classified ad. Which do you think will bring you more business?

Including banner ads with content

It's critical that you negotiate this after you have already established an agreement to exchange content based links. Doing this beforehand may cause uncertainty with your prospect, as they may feel you are just trying to push your product onto their customers. Remember: The business owner is more interested in protecting his customer base than promoting you and even in most cases making a profit from your product.

After you have agreed to exchange content, you may like to suggest adding a banner ad somewhere in the middle of the content or at the end. Make it a small banner. Explain to your new exchange partner that including a banner can not only improve the appearance of the article (if it's a nice looking banner), but that it can significantly increase the number of orders generated from the article.

Go on to mention that once a visitor reads the information he is usually excited to learn more. Including a banner ad just increases the number of people who may investigate it further by clicking on the ad.

If your exchange partner objects, just include the usual links embedded in the article and at the end.

Real-Life examples

We approached a company selling software that related to our customer base. We asked them if they would place a link on their site in return for a link placed on our site. The answer came back "no." So we sent another email asking them if they would like to offer a downloadable eBook on their site that includes links back to their site and also additional links that link to ours. The answer came back "yes."

This now became a content based link, not a link exchange. The content made it valuable. A link on it's own is usually not considered valuable. Links that include content, software, tools, etc. - now that's valuable!

From zero to hundreds of subscribers using only link exchanges

Another membership site we launched went from zero to hundreds of subscribers (non-paying - revenue is generated from back-end products), using no other form of advertising but a high quality content exchange.

Our site was listed on the corresponding website under their resource section. This resource section included a small write-up about us and a link directed to our sign-up page.

Having your website listed in the "Resource" section of another website can be a huge traffic generator - providing that the resource page is targeted and contains actual descriptions and not just URLs.

How was this done?

1. We set up a site offering downloadable audio content.

2. We offered free audio content as a resource to website owners, not as a link exchange.

3. It's not required to even mention the words "link exchange". Focus on providing a service, the link will follow automatically.

Setting up a content based linking strategy

Step #1: Seek out potential linking partners

Apart from searching for your keyword under Google, take some time to check out the sites that link to any competitors or similar products/services to yours. You'll probably end up with a more responsive list, as these sites are already in the habit of linking to a particular kind of product.

You can check out your competitors' links and the quality of links by downloading this free software tool:

CheckYourLinkPopularity.com

Step #2: Finding more potential linking partners

Check out some of the sites that link to your competitor and see who links to them. You can continue this chain until the links lose their relevance to your site.

Step #3: Make a list of potential link partners

Using a spreadsheet or notepad, keep a track of the top sites you would like to link to.

Step #4: Contact linking partners that have the same or higher page rank than you

Using the example letter above, customize each email and send it out to your list.

Step #5: Create the necessary resource

Once a website owner agrees to the link exchange, put together the case study, article, ebook, etc. with his affiliate link to your site included.

Tips:

Don't just link to a site for the sake of getting a link in return. Your outbound links to other sites need to be considered valuable to your readers. Don't clutter links and resources by providing useless destinations.

Don't forget to use free press services to obtain high quality links. Below are a list of places we use:

- FreeSticky.com

- Pressbox.co.uk

- PRweb.com

- AllMerchants.com

- WebDevInfo.com

- InternetNewsBureau.com

- Demc.com

Building quality inbound links to your website can be a source of ongoing high volume traffic. Find the time to set it up. You'll see the benefits of your time for years to come.

CHAPTER 11

Getting and keeping subscribers

Learn the latest methods for finding new subscribers, target marketing and traffic building strategies. Once you've got them, here's how to keep them...

90% of successful websites we've researched use these methods for generating new customers and new subscribers...

- Joint Ventures

- Pay-per-click: Overture, Google, Findwhat, etc.

- Search Engine Optimization

- Link exchanges

- Co-registration

- Ezine advertising

How many of these promotions are you using?

Once you've got subscribers, how do you keep them?

Apart from providing good service and content, there are 2 ways to keep subscribers coming back.

1. Soap Opera Marketing: Have you ever watched "Days of our Lives" or "The Bold and the Beautiful"? Come on, you can admit it. I'm not a fan, but they use good marketing.

Anyway, if you haven't seen an episode you might like to watch one, just to see what they do at the end of every single show! Do you know what they do? At the end of each show they leave the story unfinished - just as it's getting good - they leave you hanging - they give you teasers of what's to come. Why? Because you and everyone else will want to come back tomorrow just to see what happened. And it works! Just look at how long these shows have been running. (Days of Our Lives has been running for a staggering 40 years...!) We call this, "soap opera marketing." Be careful, don't get hooked and then blame me.

You can and should use this same marketing strategy. Simply create a section in your members' only area where you can tell subscribers what's 'coming soon' or 'what's in the future.' We use this method on all 3 of our membership sites. This will keep your subscribers wanting more. It's one of the most important ways of creating a steady cashflow from recurring subscribers.

2. Beyond content: Ever heard the saying "content is king"? Is it really? Well that depends on your niche. However, I can guarantee you one thing... even if your site is predominantly content, you will get far more sign-ups and far more re-subscribers if you offer tools. This might just be

simple templates (like we mentioned at the beginning of this article), or even tools they can download (those you didn't even create, but which you found).

You see, when you offer a tool or some kind of service, you are creating an interactive subscriber. They have the chance to do something other than just read. An interactive subscriber will be worth far more to you than one who simply reads. That's a fact!

Not only will tools allow you to turn your subscribers into interactive members, but the members will want to return to keep using the tools. More than likely they will also tell others about the tools or services available on your site. It's a powerful concept and one you should plan from the start.

Offering tools as an incentive to subscribe to your site will also dramatically increase conversion rates.

So how do you come up with a tool? Simple, ask yourself what tools do I currently use, or what tools would my subscribers need to help them do whatever it is that I'm teaching?

If you can't find an appropriate tool online, then try getting one created. Think it will cost a fortune? Think again. Places like www.rentacoder.com allow you to place a project online and have programmers bid on it. You'll be surprised how inexpensive it is to get an application or tool made for you.

One of our new software tools is going to be a membership site creator package. Our programmer is working on it as I write (see back of book for details).

CHAPTER 12

Find new leads online using low cost - high response Ezine Advertising

Internet marketers have been using ezine advertising for years to reach thousands of potential customers overnight and for very little cost. Here's how they do it....

What is an Ezine? Ezine stands for electronic magazine. There are millions of them online, with just about any topic you can imagine. Total subscribers for a single ezine can be from a few hundred, to hundreds of thousands. Ezines vary in design, many of them are simple text, others are html.... they include graphics and varying font sizes, etc. Both work well.

3 Reasons why Ezine advertising is effective

1. It's low cost. You don't have to sell much, or sign-up many people to break even.

2. You can reach your exact target market... sometimes called 'niche marketing.' You can narrow down exactly who you want to speak to, and target your message towards them. This alone is a power marketing strategy.

3. Good ezine publishers have loyal readers. These readers are looking forward and expecting to receive the publication. A well worded ad in this kind of ezine can pull instant traffic. Usually rates for ezine advertising vary between $10 - $150. Price varies depending on whether or not there are other ads included in the ezine or whether it is a solo ad.

Choosing the right ezine

Finding the right ezine to advertise in isn't hard. However, you need to do a bit of research in order to choose one that fits your target market. To do this, simply subscribe to a number of ezines on the topic you want to focus on. Take some time to study the information they send out, what other kinds of ads are running, what products they are promoting, etc. You're looking for 3 things.

1. The ezine must contain information that is relevant: For example, if you're targeting people who want to start their own home based business, don't advertise in an ezine that is providing solutions for home based business owners. It might be a related field, but you're looking for a specific and hungry market. You want to advertise in an ezine that is educating their readers on starting a home business - topics like: How to choose the right business, how to start your own home business, etc. Although both publications might generate a response... the more you identify

your correct target market, the more success you will have.

2. Look for ads that constantly run, that are similar to what you are offering. It's highly likely if a business continues to run the same ad over and over, then it's working.

3. Avoid ezines that don't offer good content. Ezines that just blast a sales message each time or are filled with ads should be avoided.

Finding ezines to advertise in

To find ezines, visit the following ezine directories.

http://ezine-universe.com/
http://www.homeincome.com/search-it/ezine/
http://new-list.com/search/
http://www.ezine-dir.com/

Or just search websites online and sign-up to their bulletins. After receiving a few, email the publisher about advertising in their ezine.

Tip: Would you like to get published in an ezine for free? Try submitting articles to targeted ezines. Getting published can bring in a ton of instant traffic.

CHAPTER 13

Setting up a Joint Venture/Viral Marketing combination to market Your Membership site

Marry these two powerful marketing techniques and you'll have the perfect overnight - zero cost lead generating system. The trick is in knowing which order to use them, and how to set up your 'viral marketing engine.' Or in other words, getting people to pass on the information once you enter your target market's community. We'll cover how to do both.

Joint Venture Marketing Defined

If you will learn and use this one method alone, you'll never be short of leads, customers or traffic. Joint venture marketing is about building your business using "other peoples' customers," with their complete endorsement. JV marketing can build your subscriber list, secure lifetime customers and recruit others to sell your products for you! It is the process of getting others to tell "their customers" about your product or service.

Better yet, not just telling them - but RECOMMENDING and endorsing your product. My very first joint venture (back in 1994) made me $13,000 in profits within a few months. Online, this method of marketing is even easier and more effective.

With JV Marketing....

- You don't need to rank high in search engines!
- You don't need to run ads!
- You don't need to build a mailing list!
- You don't need a high-traffic website!
- You don't need to buy lists!
- You don't need an advertising budget!

.... That's joint venture marketing!

In fact, if you know how to send an email you can do Internet Joint Venture Marketing.

Fortune 500 companies use Joint Venture Marketing all the time. For example: Have you ever gone to McDonalds or Burger King and received a Disney Toy from the latest Disney movie? That's a joint venture between Burger King and Disney. They are sharing a common customer, therefore benefiting from each other's marketing efforts.

Here are some of the responses we got from business owners wanting to JV with us. This was after we contacted them via email.

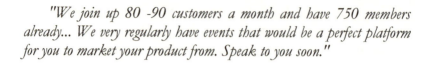

"We join up 80 -90 customers a month and have 750 members already... We very regularly have events that would be a perfect platform for you to market your product from. Speak to you soon."

"I have read your website info and it would be good to further discuss this unique opportunity networking to my clients"

There are many different Joint Venture combinations. For now we'll focus on ezine (online newsletters) Joint Venture Marketing. If you want a sudden burst of traffic to your site, this is the way to do it.

3 of the most common Joint Ventures

There are basically 3 types of joint ventures you'll be setting up.

1.   One of you supplies the product or service. The other provides the customer/prospect list. You both split the profits (usually 50/50).

2.   You and your joint venture partner do promotions for each other's products to each of your customer/prospect lists.

3.   Sometimes you can set up a joint venture where your product or service is free (has to be really wanted by your target market).

Then you can offer a product they can buy as a follow-up. You have to be careful with this one... make sure your

JV partner is aware of what you're doing. We've been able to successfully set up a couple of these (it's a highly successful deal). For example, we recently launched a website where we let our target market join for free and listen to online audio training. We've set up a joint venture where our partners can direct their customers to our site. We are providing a valuable tool to both parties. We generate profit not on the service but on the follow-up (backend) product. We offer featured products all with the free service. It's a very soft sell approach.

Amplifying the success of Joint Venture Sales

When putting together a JV try to keep in mind the customer as well. Although this isn't always necessary, you will get more sales if you make a special offer to the customer/prospect list.

Ideally you want to create a win/win/win situation. That means; you win, because you get product exposure and sales. The other business wins, because they get profits from the sale (or a chance to offer something to your customers). The customer wins, because they get a discount or special deal because they purchased through the company they're already associated with.

Also, the best JV you can do is when the ezine owner endorses your product. If you write the endorsement for your potential JV partner then you'll have a much better chance of him plugging it straight into his ezine list.

Finding JV partners

Step One

Before you start looking for JV partners, find out where your target market lives. Where do they buy similar products? Where do they go for information? Whose advice do they listen to? Finding out this information will lead you to your JV partners. You'll want to JV with the people who 'talk' to your target market. It's as simple as that!

Here's a simple example: Decide on the industry you want to target, (eg. health, business, martial arts, etc). For example: Let's say you want to market to "Work-At-Home Mothers".

Step Two

To search for websites in that area: go to: http://www.google.com and type in "work at home moms" Go through a lot of the websites to get a feel for the market. You are looking for websites that offer articles or an ezine. Make a note of each website and subscribe to the ezine.

Step Three

Pick the websites that you feel would best suit your target market. For example: Look for websites offering advice to mothers trying to start a home based business. Check their ranking using http://www.alexa.com. A site with a traffic ranking of 100,000 or under is considered very good. For example, Yahoo! Ranks #1, meaning the most visited website. Alexa will also give you the site owner's details. You can now personalize the email. Sometimes you can also find out the owner's name by going to www.betterwhois.com

Step Four

Send a personalized email to each website owner. We've found it best not to try and tell everything in one go. You want to initiate dialogue first - a conversation. Then you can proceed with the entire offer.

Your email should contain at least 3 points of personalization. This might include... the person's name, website name, where you found the site, the name of their ezine, name of their product or service, how long they have been in business, etc. This will prove to them that you're not just spamming them and hundreds of others like them.

Template Email: Email we have used to set up joint venture deals

Hello (first name - if available),

I was just looking at your ------------ website. We found it on Google, under "work at home moms." I would like to offer your ---------- system to my business customers.

I market a -------. All of my customers are interested in increasing their income.

As part of a promotional offer - I would like to talk to you about recommending your ------ website to my customers, and vice versa.

You can take a look at my corporate site by going to: http://www.yourwebsite.com

Looking forward to your reply.

Warmly,
<your name>

Getting the deal

Once you've got a response to your email, you now need to make an offer. This is where you can make or break the deal. Here are some rules to follow:

1. Don't get greedy. Let your partner be greedy. I once lost, what would have been a huge deal with an internationally known martial artist (a multi-millionaire), because I made it too hard for him, and I wanted to keep most of the profit. The deal never happened. If I had kept it simple and let him keep at least 50% of the profits – we both would have made a lot of money. So offer your JV partner at least 50% of the profits. Especially if they are the one who will promote it (as was the case with my example).

2. Understand that the greatest profit potential is in the backend. Once you have secured a customer, you can continue to sell to them. So even if you make nothing on the first sale... your revenue will come in the backend.

3. With that said, your joint venture partner will also know that the profit is in the backend... so include a way for them to profit on backend sales as well. Although this might not be as high. Maybe a 30% share in backend products.

4. Don't make them work for it. That means, have your endorsement letters written, your ads ready, and their affiliate links in place (simple affiliate software will handle this task). They shouldn't have to spend hours rolling out your project. Plug and play... that's what you're looking for.

5. Make sure you've tested your advertising copy (although this is not always necessary). If your ad or endorsement letter isn't good, your JV partner won't

run it. They've got to protect their credibility. Is your product of high standard? Your product must be good. If not, you shouldn't be selling it. Send your potential JV partner a copy of your product. Prove that it's good.

Viral Marketing defined:

Viral marketing is where one customer passes it onto many other people, usually via email. It's basically word of mouth marketing amplified.

So how do you make your product viral?

Whenever you create a product you should be creating it to become viral. In some case your product can't be viral, especially if you're offering certain services. But you can still use viral marketing. We've designed simple online tools that become viral... those tools become our viral marketing engine, leading people back to our original product. Our latest viral marketing tool is a free website offering audio training. Simple interviews uploaded to a site in MP3 format. The idea went viral before we could even finish the site!

Here are some other ways to initiate a viral marketing component...

1. Affiliate programs. The simplest way to make a product viral is to offer an affiliate program. This is how network marketing companies become so big.

2. Ebooks. It's getting harder with ebooks because there are so many around. However, if you have good content, along with a great topic and headline, this will still work. If there is a real life copy of the book available for purchase, it will give a high perceived value to a digital format.

3. Simple tools and software are great viral marketing tools. (eg: Companies release fully functional software with some limited features. Users have to pay for the extra features). Try releasing a free tool that fits the same market for your primary product. Then include links and details in the free tool, back to your other product. The tool needs to be useful and wanted.

4. When people use your product, others can see what it is and know where to get it. For example: Our website that offers services for marketers of noni juice... when other marketers see this they can click on a link to get the same service. So the more the product is out there, the more people see it and come back to us. Hotmail.com perfected this. Every time an email was sent, it included a signature file showing the receiver how to get the same, and so on, and so on. Massive rapid growth!

How to marry Joint Venture Marketing and Viral Marketing

Both of these methods are similar. When you set up a JV you are getting someone who communicates (and has credibility) on a large scale to your target market. This is the guy that, once he talks, your target market listens. Once you've got the JV partner to release the announcement, you will do so much better if you then have your target market talk about your product to each other. This will generate long term business and leads for you.

One of our sites gets leads and customers every day. Simply because we did a JV and then it turned viral. Every day our new customers tell another potential customer about us. We've never had to pay for advertising on that product.

Summary Tips

The more joint ventures you do, the easier it will get. You will get more and more partners who will introduce you to other partners. Don't be intimidated by very successful companies or people. We've done deals with national companies, multi-millionaires, magazine publishers and small home based businesses. All of these deals have been valuable and profitable. They have lead to other joint ventures that we hadn't even considered.

Try other forms of contact. Follow-up an email with a fax. Try a phone call. You'll be surprised who you can get through to, if you word your email correctly. I've spoken to some famous people, and put together joint ventures with millionaires... even when I had nothing - no money, no customers, just the idea or a product and a website. Become a deal maker!

Real-Life Case Study #4

'Disney style' illustrator sells paid subscriptions using Word-of-Mouse marketing

DrawShop.com sells annual memberships to their downloadable database of 'Disney style' illustrations using nothing but word-of-mouse marketing. Poul Carlsen shares how he runs his successful membership site from Denmark, without spending a dime on advertising.

Poul Carlsen, founder of DrawShop.com, is a web illustrator and well known throughout the webmaster/clipart communities. Poul's story begins in 1958 in the country of Denmark, where he was born.

Turning a passion into profits

Poul first began illustrating in 1974 when he was just 16

years old, working for a non profit organization. Through the years he refined and honed his skills. He eventually started working for a Danish company, where he learned about marketing brochures and other graphic layouts.

When Poul was 25 years old he took his next big step. He began working for a large company called "Sis-International". He opened their department of graphics advertising, creating their folders, price lists and brochures. All the while Poul was also working from his home, privately, selling drawings to companies and magazines. When Poul was 30 years old, he quit the job which he had created for himself at "Sis-International," to follow his dream of starting his own company, "PC-illustration & Reklame".

Becoming self-employed

Poul was now able to work full time for himself, selling his work exclusively to companies, advertising bureaus, and editors in Denmark. In 1997, Poul launched his now famous DrawShop.com to expose his work not just to companies, but to the world.

How to run a word-of-mouse membership site: Questions & answers

1. Poul, what is www.DrawShop.com all about?

DrawShop.com - is a place where people who are working with advertising or media can order customized graphics to complete their advertising promotion.

These Graphical illustrations are used in media, websites and printed promotional materials. Companies with graphic jobs, who have a limited budget, come to us for help. This is where our membership site offer is a great way for businesses to get quality graphics for a small investment.

2. How did the idea for www.DrawShop.com come about?

It all started in 1995 - when the Internet was growing fast. I started thinking there must be a market for my kind of work outside of Denmark.

I was lucky enough to register a good domain name: "DrawShop.com" - I got in before other graphic companies and web developers tried to register it.

I was right with my idea! People worldwide went crazy with my talent to draw in the special "Disney Style." That's what makes my membership site and me unique.

When I started DrawShop.com, I didn't provide customized jobs as a service - we only sold pre-designed graphics. I quickly realized I was missing back-end sales by not providing customized work. So I added this service to my site.

The Membership download section was first started a year ago. That really improved my cashflow, as membership orders for DrawShop.com rolled in.

3. How many new subscribers do you normally get each day or week?

I can tell you, on a normal day we get about 2-4 new subscribers. (That's about US$490 - US$980 per week of new sales. Not including recurring billings or back-end profits from customized work).

It's important to note that a lot of our profits come from back-end sales. Members are happy with our work and sometimes want personalized artwork. We are able to charge members around $500 for an illustration.

So the initial annual fee of $35 is just the start. As many business owners know, the real profits can come from additional customer sales.

Author's Note: We found the same was true with one of our membership sites. We added another service that members could purchase in addition to paying their membership fee. As a result, monthly profits doubled.

Existing customers are 5 times more likely to buy from you than a new prospect.

Avoid too many offers, as members are already paying subscription fees. However, back-end marketing can certainly be profitable. Even to the point of doubling cash flow.

Poul does his back-end promotions very successfully.

---

4. You charge an annual fee. Have you found this to be the best payment option for your site?

Yes, the annual fee works well.

A lot of people buy graphics online, maybe one or two at a time. But why pay $10 for 2 graphics, when you can get our entire range on DrawShop.com, for only $35 per year? And this includes new additions made throughout the year.

5. Have you tested other payment options, like a monthly amount?

No, I feel in my case, it's better to offer an annual subscription rather than weekly or monthly options.

When visitors or subscribers see the graphical content continually growing and the price remains constant - well, it's a good reason to return and take out or renew a membership.

6. How do you process credit cards?

We use PayPal.com and WorldPay.com, as third party processors.

7. Who is your target market?

Our target market breaks down into the following:

- Small business owners

- Webmasters

- People who work in advertising

- Layout designers for promotions materials

- People trying to start a business or launch/upgrade a website

8. What kind of active promotional activities do you participate in, to get subscribers?

- Word-of-mouse marketing / Joint venture marketing.

- Search engine marketing - especially with Google.

In the past I've purchased targeted visitors, with not much success.

Finally, we use our affiliate program with great success. There are a lot of people out there searching for good affiliate programs. I know ours works because we pay out hundreds of dollars in commissions.

9. Out of those promotional activities mentioned, where do most of your visitors come from?

- Google

- Word-of-mouse marketing (having links under mascot illustrations on other peoples' sites... that lead back to my site).

- Affiliate partners

- Link or banner exchangers

10. How do you go about putting together a word-of-mouse or joint venture campaign? What do you say to get a potential partner interested?

I offer a free membership to Drawshop for potential partners.

In return, I ask them to place my banner ad on their website for one year. The site must generate at least 12000 unique visitors per year for them to keep the free membership.

Secondly I also offer a free main graphic, a "mascot" - The web owner must add a credit link to my site. The "mascot" and corresponding link must appear on their home page. The link must never be deleted from the website - as long they use the graphics.

This particular method of link exchanging of word-of-mouse marketing brings a lot of traffic. My only cost is providing a quality graphic for my partner.

11. Are there any other promotions that you have found to be effective in bringing you paid subscribers?

Since the beginning of 2004, I have consistently added a new illustration every week. It's important to keep fresh content on membership sites.

This has caused quite a stir. People talk. As a result of this word-of-mouth marketing method I've been fortunate enough to get a lot of extra traffic. In fact, traffic has increased 300% since January.

12. What software do you use to manage your membership subscribers?

We have our own staff here at DrawShop. Our IT guy developed a customized script for us. The script manages both our affiliate and membership sections. So we don't have to outsource software. It's kept within our own organization. This gives us full control.

13. Have you tested various pricing to find the best combination?

The way I determine pricing, is to search out the typical prices on the internet for similar graphics.

Then I ask people (friends, family and customers), how much they would pay for a service like this. The most common answer was US$35.

I have not tried changing the price. I believe this price will suit any budget - private as well as commercial.

14. You have a high paying affiliate program. Has this helped you acquire many affiliates?

Yes absolutely. The affiliate program is an important way to get subscriptions. I think a membership site must include an affiliate program to become a great success.

15. How is your retention? Is there anything that you do in particular to keep subscribers coming back and renewing or keeping their subscriptions?

You work hard to get members. To keep them you need to upload new products/content every week. Then subscribers will stay with you, or come back to renew their membership.

A lot of our members re-subscribe because of the amount of new illustrations. They may not always renew at the end of the term, but they sure come back for a look when new content is added.

16. What kind of strategy do you use to separate yourself from your competitors?

I simply listen to my customers. A lot of the time they will make special requests for specific content.

A lot of the content on Drawshop is from sketches of customized work, requested by an organization. It's common to do several different sketches to find the right one. And some companies determine that none are "the right one". These 'left-over' sketches are now put to good use.

Since half the work is already done, I complete the sketch as a final graphic and upload it to my members area.

So my work never goes to waste on DrawShop.com

17. Do subscribers receive any other additional services?

No, only the downloadable illustrations in the members' area.

18. What have you found to be the best way to convert traffic into paying customers?

Easy and clear copy on the main page. I believe short copy on the home page works well. Not too cluttered. Have a good banner, (company logo, etc.) to make your site look professional.

19. What kind of conversion rate do you have for your site? (Unique visitors to paying customers)

It's about 1-2 new subscribers per 1000 visitors. Or a 1 - 2% conversion rate.

20. What would be the most important thing you would say to someone trying to start and promote his own membership site?

Service and Service - if a customer has a question, do what you can to help him/her on the same day. I try to answer support questions within hours. I don't leave customers waiting for a week. Fast responses are key to any good business on the Internet.

Part 4
Advanced marketing and promotional strategies

CHAPTER 14

How to use Google Adwords to start getting subscribers overnight

Pay less on any keyword. Rank higher than others paying more than you. These tips will show you how to take full advantage of how Google.com ranks and charges for advertising.

What is "Google Adwords?"

Whenever someone does a search using Google, Google will bring up a page showing an index of websites. On the right side of the page, you will notice green boxed ads, those are Google Ads.

In this section we're going to cover how to increase your traffic using Google adwords, while reducing your costs. We'll look at paying less per click on an ad, at the same time ranking higher than competitors.

Google is different from other search engines. The way other search engines work, with regard to paying for listings (pay-per-click), is that whoever bids the highest amount for a keyword, will rank the highest. Meaning whoever has the biggest wallet wins.

Google on the other hand works on a combination of popularity (how many people click on your ad) and how much you are willing to pay. Which means, if you have a popular ad you can actually rank higher than someone paying more than you.

What are some of the mistakes people make when running a Google ad campaign?

There are 3 main mistakes people make when running ads on Google:

1. They choose the wrong kind of keyword. Or focus the wrong ad to the wrong market.

2. They don't select enough keywords. They feel they can just run an ad with a few keywords and their work is done.

3. They don't track the sales generated from the keywords. For example, a particular keyword might generate great traffic but no sales. Another keyword might generate a small amount of traffic but lots of sales. Which ad would you prefer to be spending money on?

* Google.com provides a free ad tracking tool with your account.

How do you make sure you choose the right keyword?

Choosing the right keyword is critical to your success. You'll need to pick a keyword or keyphrase that is common to your target market. For example, if you're selling sunglasses for babies, then some keywords you might use would be: "baby sunglasses," "sunglasses for babies," "infant sunglasses," "baby's sunglasses," etc. It's any phrase you think your target market will use when searching online. A good way to choose keywords is to think about what you would type in to look for a particular product.

You'll then need to test the keywords in your actual campaign. Google (and other search engines) provide suggestion tools for additional keywords and phrases which people are searching on. Another good place to find keywords is to go to: **www.inventory.overture.com**

How many keywords should you use?

It's not uncommon for business people to come to me and say, "we're not getting the kind of results we expected from our Google Adwords campaign." The first question I ask them is, "how many keywords are you running?" The response is usually around 5, 10 or maybe even 20. Running that number of keywords is not enough. There are two reasons for this:

1. You are covering a very narrow market if they're the only keywords you can come up with.

2. You can't have tested too many keywords if that's all you're running.

You need to be testing hundreds of keywords at a time, until you find the ones that work best. You may only start with 5 or 20 keywords, but as you research more words and use the suggestion tools you will quickly build a list of hundreds. The keywords that work will then become apparent. We've had keywords that we thought would work well, but bombed. Conversely we've had keywords which we thought weren't too relevant to our market, yet they pulled in the highest number of sales. There is no way we could know this if we didn't run hundreds of keywords and let statistics make the decision.

What do you do when you find a great keyword, but competitors are bidding very high on it – meaning your ad doesn't even show up until the 10th page?

There are 3 things you can do:

1. You can look for keyphrases rather than keywords. For example, let's say you want the keyword "golf," but it's too competitive – you could use a keyphrase instead, such as "professional golf clubs."

2. You can run the keyword anyway but pay a low price. As your ad gets clicks it becomes more and more popular. You can then increase the amount you're paying for the ad, but because it's already popular you will in fact pay less than someone whose ad isn't as popular. It's a way of climbing up the Google adwords ladder.

3. Another popular method is to front load your ad. Simply put, you pay the high bid rate up-front to your ad ranked high, but only for a short period of time. Just enough time to get you a popular click rate. Once you have a high click rate, you suddenly cut back your bid amount. If you're ad is well written and has a high click rate, you can maintain your high position while paying less, as your ad is being supported by your popularity.

What strategies do you use to encourage people to click on your ad, making it popular?

I see Google ads like classified ads in a newspaper. Whoever writes the best classified ad will get the most phone calls. Likewise, whoever writes the best Google ad will get the most clicks. To explain how to write a good ad is a whole other topic, but the easiest thing to do is to just study other ads, online and offline. Here are some tips to help you get started:

- Write a great headline that promises a strong benefit to your reader. Also take some time to look back at the Google ad example we wrote earlier in the book.
- Don't try to tell a story in a classified ad. Just list the most important points one after the other.
- Where possible use your most popular keyword in the headline and body of the ad. This will also help your ad rank higher, as Google places more importance (ranks you higher) on ads that contain the specific keyword you are targeting.

CHAPTER 15

Highly effective Viral Marketing Technique for Membership Sites

A unique Viral marketing strategy that boosted our traffic and increased paying subscriptions by more than 120% on the same day. This is how we set it up.

H ave you noticed the marketing shift with the Internet? As more and more people move over to broadband, websites and content will become very multimedia orientated (it's already happening). It won't replace text content, but it will be a valuable addition!

Before we reveal any of the strategies used in this viral marketing campaign, let's take a look at the real results – the stats on the following page:

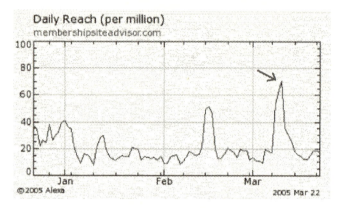

As you can see from the diagram above, the highest traffic came around mid March. So what has caused the sudden leap in traffic…? An eVideo!

Video Viral marketing

Just like in the "real world," video has a high perceived value. If it's a video, it's worth a lot more than text or audio (usually). And because it's visual it's more likely to be passed on.

Studies have proven that video and/or visual content increase sales and also increase the retention level of knowledge about the product.

So did it improve our sales?

The day we released our eVideo we had over a 120% increase in paying subscribers. That's right, we more than doubled our subscription rate that day and for many, many days after the release of the video. In fact, it was one of our highest cashflow weeks for this membership site.

Now it just wasn't the extra traffic that caused the boost in paying subscriptions (although it certainly helped), but it was also because videos can give you instant credibility.

For example, which would hold up better in a court of law, the testimony of a witness, or the actual security video capturing the whole event? Videos have instant credibility and trust (except for some media stations).

Conversely, that's why many people fall into the trap when watching TV.

They think that if it's on TV it must be true.

People tend to trust what they can see with their own eyes. We had people emailing who had been on our free bulletin list for some time, saying that they signed up because they enjoyed the eVideo and wanted to learn more.

And sometimes things just have to been seen – either to be believed or to be understood.

We recently hired a programmer to develop a new software application for us. It wasn't until we video taped a whiteboard presentation (just me standing there drawing on a whiteboard), that he fully understood what we wanted and how we wanted it to work.

Trying to tell the programmer via "words" or even audio just wasn't working. But a simple 10 minute video clip explained the entire project.

An eVideo just doesn't have to be about explaining the product. You can also interview satisfied customers to create a highly credible sales campaign, which is also viral marketing newsworthy.

For eVideos that are just recordings of your monitor, you can download the latest version of "Windows Media Encoder" for free. This application will allow you to record your screen movements and turn it into a video. It's great for training tutorials.

Free download link:

www.hitsquad.com/smm/programs/Windows_Media_Encoder/

Unleashing your eVideo marketing virus

What's the fastest way to get your eVideo out to the world? Below are some useful methods for launching your eVideo virus in a short amount of time.

Remember that to launch a successful viral marketing campaign, you need to go to the source that supplies information to the "hive" (your target market). Your idea then needs to be encapsulated in a medium (an eVideo in this case), it then needs to be exciting, unique and/or funny enough for people within the "hive" to a pass it on.

How to get maximum exposure for your eVideo

- Blast it out to your in-house list first. And ask them to pass it onto friends if they found it useful.

- Contact potential joint venture partners and offer the eVideo as a resource for their site. Invite them to use it as a premium on other offers or to blast out to their list. I've actually had many people email me wanting to use our eVideos as content on their site. These unsolicited offers are common when it involves an eVideo. For large JV partners you may even want to mention their site, or product in your video. This almost guarantees they will blast out your eVideo.

- Post your eVideo (with some text) onto various forums in your related industry. Do it in a non-blatant way. It should be content orientated, not an advertisement.

- Turn it into a CD or DVD and sell it on eBay.

- If it's professional enough, you may also want to sell it on Amazon.com by turning it into a larger DVD production. We are in the process of doing that right now, with another project.

Check list: How to structure your eVideo presentation

1. Set up a web page containing the video. You want your video to be on a website. You don't want it being forwarded as an attachment, as this will take up too much bandwidth, not to mention many spam filters will remove it. A website link is much easier for people to forward onto their friends and associates.

2. Add a "tell a friend" feature on the web page containing the eVideo. You can even use the free "tell a friend" tool used at www.Bravenet.com. You want to encourage people to watch the eVideo and then pass it on.

3. Include teasers on the page. For example you might like to say something like: "Did you enjoy this video? To access more videos like this click here." This link would direct them to your membership site sales/sign-up page or home page. This soft sell approach has a high sales conversion rate.

4. The eVideo itself should have your website address shown somewhere on the video. Preferably at the beginning and end.

5. Try to make the eVideo as part of a series. This will encourage viewers to want more. If you have the talent and skills, you could even include a small 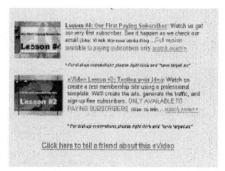 commercial about your membership site at the beginning of the eVideo. For a perfect example, check out the news video casts on yahoo.

http://story.news.yahoo.com/news

Each video starts with a commercial. You can do a simplified version of this with your own videos:

Does it have to be "Real-Life" video?

No, but real-life video creates far more trust and excitement. However, if appearing on video just isn't your thing, you do have two other choices.

You can have someone else appear on the video. Like an expert in your field.

Or...

You can just create a video screen capture of your computer screen, or an animated PowerPoint presentation.

Do you have an idea for an eVideo in your business?

What could you demonstrate, or teach to your target market? Go ahead and create a viral marketing eVideo!

CHAPTER 16

Double your income adding a "shop" to your membership site

"...there's just something about launching an online shop that causes a buying frenzy"

Selling physical products like CDs, DVDs, books, software, etc via your membership site can boost your cashflow overnight. In fact, we recently created an online "shop outlet" for one of our membership sites that almost doubled our income this month alone - and we only  just launched it. Learn how we acquired the rights to bestselling unique products (one company wanted US$5,000 upfront - we quickly had them drop this fee completely), how we set-up fulfillment, and now how we plan to release our own book.

Just a few weeks ago we launched an online shop as an extension or back-end to one of our other membership sites. In the process we were able to set up several joint ventures, move thousands of dollars worth of products within a few days, have our shop promoted for us and acquire the rights to top selling products.

For a long time I have only sold digital products. But it was exciting to once again return to print media - especially with the windfall of cashflow.

When you've established a relationship with your clients, there's just something about launching an online shop that causes a buying frenzy. And from what we've found, it seems to be amplified if you're moving from a digital product to a physical product.

Not only was the online shop an extension of our membership site, but we used it to set up several joint ventures, which is a key part of the entire exercise. In a minute you'll learn how you can use your "shop outlet" to set up joint ventures even if your membership site has little or no subscribers.

The shop was launched without a single product in stock. Products were either pre-publications, or other people's products. Thanks to the technology of "print on demand" we are able to produce professional products as orders surge in.

This kind of technology frees you from expensive inventory, and major set up fees.

Why physical products in the digital information age?

Often clients want instant digital products. However, when it comes to major courses, products such as DVDs, CDs, Books, Software, etc., have a much higher perceived value. And you've got to admit... it's still nice to get a package in the mail now and then.

Physical products carry a certain kind of credibility, and if you already have an established client base, a tangible product can become a wanted item.

Here's how we set it up, from product selection to order fulfillment:

Selecting your products:

Would you rather sell an unknown product or a proven bestseller? Which do you think would give you the chance of generating immediate cashflow?

Top sellers - you need to locate the top selling products in your industry. Should you decide to create a shop with your products exclusively, you will still want to emulate other best selling products.

It shouldn't be hard to find them. They will be listed on the search engines. You can find them on other peoples' sites. Many sites, particularly online stores will list their best selling products. This is vital information. They are telling you what people want to buy. It's not theory. People actually want those products.

More than likely you will already know the bestsellers - you may even own a copy.

One strategy that we have used successfully is to take several best selling ideas and package them up together to create a custom built course. Not only can this create joint venture opportunities with the authors, but it can sell as a high ticket item. In our case we were able to sell thousands of dollars worth of custom packaged products in the last few days. And we authored none of them.

Your action steps in a nutshell:

a) Select top selling products.

b) Repackage them to make an exclusive package or course.

c) Try to incorporate mixed mediums, eg. Books, DVDs, CDs, Software. Not necessarily all of them.

d) Put together the new sales copy for your exclusive program.

e) If time and skills permit, try and include at least one of your own products.

Below is a screenshot of an exclusive package we helped put together using other peoples' top selling products.

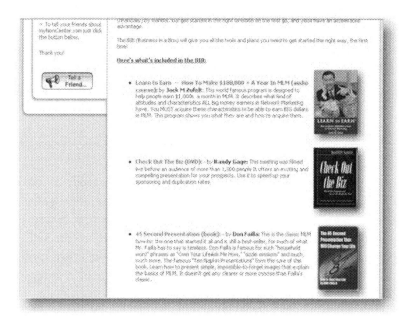

Acquiring reprint rights for top selling products at zero up-front cost:

Your success will depend on a sellable product. Before you can generate an income you must have a product to sell. There are only two ways to accomplish this:

1. Research and create it from scratch, or

2. Acquire the marketing and duplication/reprint rights to promote them.

This is how we acquired the rights to 11 top selling products with zero up-front cost.

One publishing company we contacted, who owned the rights to a particular DVD we felt would be valuable to include in a new program, asked us for US$5,000 up-front. This fee would allow us to start duplicating the DVD ourselves and pay them $1.50 royalty on each copy sold. A small royalty, big up-front fee. Keep in mind this is a top selling product.

Not wanting to fork out US$5,000 (can you imagine if we had to pay that on each of the 11 products? I'll let you do the math), we negotiated to have the entire fee dropped. It took one simple email. On the next page is an example of the email we used...

Hi ***,

Thanks for the information about your DVD.

I have spoken to one of our top associates who will be promoting the DVD. He wants to include the DVD in one of our packages. So the DVD will go out in every order we fill.

There are some concerns over the US$5,000 fee. We currently market a lot of products and have reprint rights to all of them. We've actually never had to pay an upfront fee. That leaves us with 2 options:

1. Instead of the upfront fee, maybe your royalty could be increased. What do you think?

2. We could look at purchasing it at wholesale. The problem with that is we have to pay shipping, tax, etc. Which will probably make it too expensive. But it is an option.

Failing that, we will have to replace it with another product. Unfortunately we have many products in the package and if each one charged US$5,000 we would be up for tens of thousands of dollars.

I appreciate your time. Let me know where to from here.

All my best,
Ansel

This one email had the upfront fee dropped. As an incentive, on the second email we offered a $2 royalty instead of $1.50. That's much better than a $5,000 upfront fee.

But the steps prior to this are just as important. Here's what we did:

i) First we contacted the publisher via email, indicating we were interested in marketing their product to our client base. Even if you don't have your own client base right now, in all honesty you can still offer to promote it via your associates' clients - or in other words joint venture partners. You'll notice we stated in the previous email that we would offer it to our top associates (joint venture partners), even though we have a big client base. It just adds credibility and impact.

ii) We then followed up with a phone call and spoke directly with the CEO of the company - he was in Paris at the time, but due to return the following day. We called again the next day.

iii) We negotiated the royalty and terms via email.

Where are the best places to find top sellers?

- Newspapers
- Amazon.com
- BarnesandNoble.com
- Search engines. Just observe what's being offered for sale as you search your favorite topics.
- And one of my favorites - looking at long standing ads, whether online or offline. If there is a number of ads, all running for some time, selling the same thing, good chance it's a hot product.

Setting up your shop:

The fastest way is to use a template, which we did. Our shop was up in no time, with a range of pre-publication products and products to which we acquired the rights. Below is a screenshot of the shop.

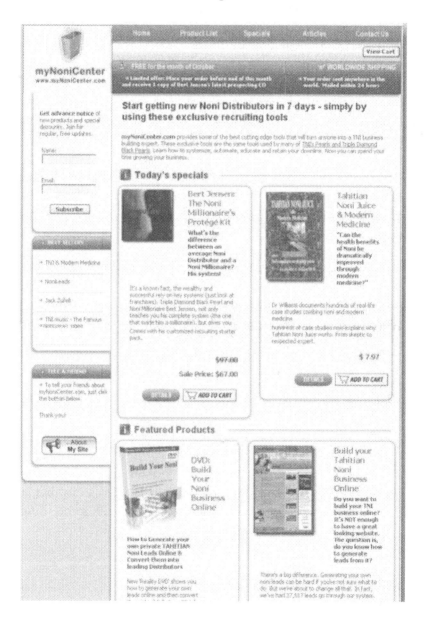

Setting up all the products was the most time consuming of all.

Order fulfillment:

Not having the time to fill orders ourselves, we needed to put in place a distribution center. There are 4 choices when it comes to distribution of tangible products

1. Do it yourself. Very time consuming.

2. Hire a fulfillment company. A good option, but there are warehouse storage fees involved, and if the package needs to be assembled (if it's made up of several books, DVDs, CDs, etc), then you will also be charged additional assembly fees.

3. If it's a simple product from the same company, you can arrange to have it drop shipped directly from the company to your client. Another good option. But it won't work here. One of our packages is made up from 5 different companies' products.

4. Hire someone to handle distribution from his home. This is a great option if set up correctly. Here's how we did it.

Hiring people to help you at zero up-front cost

I've been able to use this strategy to handle distribution centers in two different countries (US & Australia). The distribution center we set up for this particular shop is located in Las Vegas, Nevada.

Instead of paying someone (or several people) a fixed salary and benefits, which involves a lot of overheads you may not want to incur, you can hire independent contractors to work from their own home (or even from your office).

How to set it up:

1. Find someone with strong entrepreneurial spirit. Usually these kinds of people will jump at the opportunity. They may see it as their chance to become self-employed. They will normally like the idea of having the flexibility and independence of setting their own hours.

2. You can find such a person via ads, associates, friends or even relatives.

3. Offer them a percentage of sales. We have hired 3 people in total using this method. We offer 10% commission on the retail price of every product they ship.

4. You can also offer hourly rates.

5. Royalties on sales.

6. Or a fixed payment.

Structuring such an arrangement needn't be complicated. A simple letter or email stating the offer, commission and when and how payment is to be made, is usually all that's required.

The individual invoices you periodically, as an "independent contractor" or under his own business name.

Finally, make sure you have some way to check quality control of the job assigned. It's your reputation on the line.

Print on demand resources:

This is the easy part. For most of our documents we use the nearest digital printing place. In the US it's FedEx Kinkos, in Australia it's OfficeWorks or Kinkos.

For perfect bound books you may want to check out:

www.LuLu.com

They have print on demand services with no up-front fees and no minimum orders.

Another company also does print on demand books and a huge range of other merchandise. Check out...

www.CafePress.com

We are in the process of using both of these companies.

Using your online shop as a joint venture channel:

Selling someone else's product before you ask them to sell yours gives you so much more the advantage.

Here's the joint venture letter we used to set up a joint venture to promote some of our up coming products. And this deal is with a large established company. The answer came back as a resounding "yes!" Using this kind of strategy, you can hop from one deal to the next, building a network of major joint venture partners.

Having an online shop allows you to set up a huge product line and unlimited joint ventures.

Here's the letter:

Just a quick email to let you know that we are receiving a number of orders from the US and UK via our site. I'm thinking that maybe there is an opportunity to market some of your other products in the very near future.

We are always on the look out for back-end products.

Would you be interested in another joint venture in the coming months where we could promote some of your other high end products to our client base?

We are also about to release a new book and DVD course (produced in the US) on ******* (it includes some of the ****** in the industry - my company included). It may be of interest to your client base. Would that be something you might be interested in?

This simple letter just landed us a big joint venture. But it doesn't stop there. Because we contacted several authors and product developers, explaining that we were including their product in our package, we were able to have them agree to blast it to their lists. They agreed because it contained their product, even if it was just a small part of the package.

You can use this strategy to launch an online shop from scratch, even if you are starting without any client base. Simply put together a package and then have the contributing authors launch the new package out to their database. Our first windfall of sales did NOT come from our own database. We haven't even blasted it out yet.

You can be an overnight success story, by leveraging other peoples' products, and customers. Try it!

CHAPTER 17

How to raise the subscription price of your site without losing a single subscriber

"...if you want to build a membership site quickly, offer free membership to your site and then use these principles to turn it into a paid membership site... "

Increasing your subscription prices can double your income overnight. But what about the risk of losing subscribers, especially if you have free members? How do you raise the price without enraging your current members?

You've probably heard this before - one of the fastest ways to increase your revenue quickly is to increase your product's selling price. Now that's not too much of a problem if you are selling a one off product. But what do you do when you have subscribers, who are billed at set prices for certain intervals? Do you just up the price and hope you don't get too many cancellations? There is a better way...

I remember doubling my company's cashflow in one month, simply by doubling the product price. We jumped up to nearly $30,000 a month for just one product. The price change was easy because it was a one off package deal. Doing the same thing wasn't so easy when I set up my first membership site, and had to turn thousands of free subscribers into $15 a month paying subscribers.

When making changes, there's always the concern that you will lose customers, decrease your cashflow and affect future retention. With membership sites, the concern is amplified because a subscriber is usually locked in at a set price.

How to increase your subscription price and have subscribers excited to pay more

The following techniques are the same methodologies we used to turn our free membership service into a paid membership site. If you can turn free subscribers into paying subscribers you will certainly be able to use the same methods to increase revenue.

In fact, if you want to build a membership site quickly, offer free membership to your site and then use these principles to turn it into a paid membership site, just as we did.

Your mindset

First you need to have your own mindset right. What does this mean? You need to approach your price increase as a back-end product. Which means you are going to have to resell to your current subscribers. If you don't, you stand to lose a lot of what you have already built up - ongoing subscribers.

Rule #1: Never force a subscriber to pay more

How have you felt as you've watched the price of fuel go up? Did it frustrate you? I know that it has frustrated me... paying more and getting less (I've been considering purchasing a new hybrid car - that is 90% electric and 10% petrol. You only have to go to the gas station once a month instead of every week. But that's another story).

Imagine how subscribers would feel if the price was suddenly increased and they didn't have a choice in the matter. Well, unlike the necessity of fueling up your car, your subscriber will most likely cancel - at least a high percentage of them.

How do you give your subscribers a choice, and still increase the price regardless? You offer an "upgrade!"

Rule #2: The whole key to increasing your price is in the UPGRADE!

By focusing all your marketing efforts on an upgrade, you now put the power back into the hands of your subscribers. If they don't want, or can't pay any more for your subscription site, then they can stay at the current price. However, if they do want the advantages that come with upgrading they will be happy to pay the increase.

Using upgrades as an incentive to increase the price not only reduces the risk of anyone canceling but can also motivate members who do want to upgrade.

It's important to look at your membership site as a product. An upgrade must be sold to current subscribers. The upgrade must include benefits that they desperately want. You have to justify, in your members' mind that the upgrade price is more than worth it, they simply MUST have it - considering the extra benefits they will receive.

Rule #3: Give your upgrade a title or name

Your upgrade offer needs to be separate from your current subscription, creating two distinct memberships. In fact, it will help if you give the new membership upgrade a name, even if the name is just "Advanced Membership". There needs to be a clear-cut definition between the two memberships. This will add value to the advanced membership, and allow you to draw attention to one or the other simply by referring to its name.

In the case of our first membership site, everyone is considered a member. However when members become paying subscribers they are then considered "Active Members". This allows both our subscribers and us to distinguish between the two, and in turn run promotions encouraging members to become "Active Members" and the advantages associated with it.

Rule #4: Time for a new look

Redesigning your site with an all new look, will go a long way to encouraging subscribers to upgrade their membership.

A new look will make the upgrade feel justified, like buying a new tool. You expect to pay more for it than you did for your old one.

Rule #5 Write out an upgrade sales letter

When encouraging our members to upgrade from free to $15 a month we designed a simple upgrade sales letter.

You need to sell the upgrade. That's why we said in the beginning that you need to have a back-end mindset. Your upgrade is a back end product. It needs to be sold.

On the following page is the sales letter we use to turn free subscribers into paying subscribers:

Advantages of becoming an "Active Subscriber"

FACT: "If NoniLeads.com helps you find even one customer or leader, it will more than pay for itself... it already has for me."

- Ken Rolfeness, Triple Diamond Black Pearl

& NoniLeads Active Subscriber

You have now started your FREE 30 day trial of NoniLeads.com. You will have the opportunity to test the tools and learn how to operate your virtual online office and lead generating system. At anytime during your 30 day trial you can become an ACTIVE SUBSCRIBER. To become an Active Subscriber you will need to enter your credit card details. However your credit card will not be charged until after your free trial. You may also cancel at anytime if unsatisfied for any reason.

6 Reasons why you should become an Active Subscriber now

As soon as you enter your credit card details you will become an Active Subscriber. You will receive the following extra benefits:

1. You will receive the free report **"Online Lead Generation: Resources and cutting edge techniques for generating quality leads online."** This downloadable report will not only show you the top 10 methods for generating leads online. It will show you, with easy to follow instructions, what to do, how to do it, and where to go. Some of the methods shown can be set-up within 5 minutes, and best of all, most of them are FREE! Here's a list of what you'll learn:

    1. Search Engines
    2. Viral Marketing
    3. Free Classifieds
    4. Rebound Emails
    5. Banner Ads
    6. Signature Files
    7. Newsgroups
    8. Chat Rooms
    9. Ezines
    10. Link exchanges

2. **Lead generating brochures**: Professionally written and designed lead generating brochures you have the to right to print and use to build your business. These brochures will be downloadable from the Members Area as soon as you become an Active Subscriber.

3. **Instant TAHITIAN NONI Juice business info pack**: When someone requests an information pack from your website what do you sent them? Now you can download a professionally designed info pack from the Members Only Area, print it and mail to your leads. The info pack is designed to bring your qualified leads into your team in the shortest possible time.

4. **Monthly articles**: Read our monthly articles on the latest lead generating, business methods, success stories and prospecting methods. Each issue is filled with 'how-to' information.

5. **Secure your website** and continue to access the Members Only Area. To continue using your website and Members Only Area before the 30 day trial expires, you will need to become an Active Subscriber. This will ensure you don't lose your user name and any leads you've added to the system.

6. **Lead share program**: Coming soon.

These bonuses are only available to Active Subscribers. To become an Active Subscriber now, and receive all of the above advantages click the PayPal link below. You may cancel at anytime.

Here's an example of another upgrade sales letter used by the popular membership site Bravenet.com:

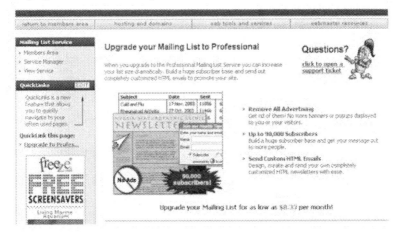

Rule #6 Give them a sneak-peek at the upgrade

Current members will become highly motivated to upgrade if they can see, but not use some of the benefits available to them if they upgrade.

For example: Our standard members can see certain tools that active members can use, but the link is not active on their site - instead it will have a caption that says, "Only available to Active Subscribers. Click here to become an Active Subscriber now". Alternatively the link will be active but when clicked on, it will take them to a sales message encouraging them to upgrade so that they can use the particular tool or read the particular content.

Bravenet.com uses the upgrade method very well. Membership to their site is free. However, if you want certain advantages when using their tools you have to upgrade to "Pro Membership". On each page they have a small box of bullet points which constantly reminds you what you are missing out on.

Rule #7 Create a pre-upgrade buzz

Not only will you be letting your subscribers know well in advance about an upgrade option, but if done correctly it can create quite a buzz. We recently did this with one of our membership sites that was going through a slow period, and the very mention of an upgrade literally shot us past our competition.

We included screen shots, detailed information and ideas we were working on. We also asked for feedback. Our subscribers truly felt like a part of the upgrade process. This type of anticipation can dramatically increase your response rate when it comes time for members to purchase an upgrade. Sequential updates and information will keep the buzz going right up until "upgrade day."

Adding a release date to the upgrade announcement will also create anticipation and excitement for subscribers.

Rule #8 Offer high quality premiums

Finally, try to include some kind of free gift when a subscriber upgrades. This free gift should have an introductory time limit. For example, "if you upgrade your subscription before Feb 14th, you get......"

Your subscribers will appreciate and even look forward to a price increase if done under the banner of an "upgrade". Try it, and watch your cashflow increase overnight...

CHAPTER 18

Setting up tiny joint ventures that have an 87% success rate

"The whole premise of this report is to encourage you to chase the smaller joint venture partners, in order to gain the experience and credibility to move onto greater things"

Imagine a JV proposal email that gets 87% of prospects saying "yes" to your offer. We'll give you that exact email. Many web business owners continue to make one major mistake when setting up JVs - Here's how to put all the odds in your favor...

When I first started putting together joint ventures I struggled. In fact, I stopped doing them. I remember getting uncomfortable when it came to asking a JV partner to market or endorse my product, after I had already agreed to market their product. I've always led with offering to promote them first, as it's usually a stronger motivator, but I always had problems bringing it back to my product.

I used to fumble around, trying to find the right way to ask them to endorse my product in return. Sometimes the correspondence would end with only my 'half hearted hinting' at the idea of my product being endorsed. But now, after trial and error, I just ask for it and I usually get it. It's a matter of learning how to do it right. Here we'll show you how to do it right.

As you've probably heard over and over again, joint ventures are one of the most powerful forms of marketing. It's a strategy that can generate immediate cashflow (our first membership site was built entirely on one JV), or increase cashflow. Yet why do so many website business owners fail to use this powerful strategy? As an example, ask yourself - "how many successful joint ventures have I put together this month?" If you're like most people, it's not many, maybe even zero. Yep marketers boast how easy it is. Why does it seem harder than it sounds? And why do so many people fail to use JVs correctly, if at all?

Here's why...

1. It takes a bit of time to set up and roll out. It can sometimes take a few weeks to settle on a joint venture proposal and then lock it in for a set release date. Usually a relationship and time frame need to be established before a JV will get the go ahead. So a bit of patience is required. In that "patience period," many small business owners lose faith that it will even work. In turn they quit using the strategy.

2. It's very rare that you will send a JV email deal to a business, agree on the terms and have them send out your sales letter to their list the next day.

It doesn't normally work like that. So many would-be joint venturing marketers feel the sting of rejections from a few larger organizations and quit trying. They quit with the feeling that it's too hard or doesn't work. This is unfortunate. By following a few simple guidelines and by focusing on mini JVs, success would be almost guaranteed.

Why mini JVs?

The whole premise of this report is to encourage you to chase the smaller joint venture partners, in order to gain the experience and credibility to move onto greater things. But in the process you will develop many contacts and increase your revenue. Imagine if each JV only brought you in 2 new sales per month. For the effort you put in, it almost doesn't seem worth it. But imagine if over the period of a month you set up 15 of these mini deals. That's now 30 new sales a month - or 360 new sales a year. Of course this is just a simplified example. Real results will vary.

If you continue to set up mini deals on a consistent basis, your business will be propelled beyond your expectations. It's our goal and part of our business plan to send at least one joint venture proposal per day (we usually try to send more), but even if it's just one - we have made that small step forward. If 20 out of the 30 say, "yes" each month and then only 5 bring us a few additional sales per month, by year's end we will have increased revenue dramatically. Do the math!

As mentioned, one of the major reasons so few marketers use JVs is because they have been rejected. But what if you were getting an 87% success rate? That would certainly change your marketing focus (and your bottom line), wouldn't it?

So how do you get an 87% success rate when so many business owners are getting rejected almost every day? The answer is easier than you think... Many business owners fail to set up joint ventures from the very beginning because they immediately approach large organizations - organizations that are far more successful and larger than themselves. Although this can certainly be done, your potential rejection is far, far higher. Unless your product is truly unique and remarkable you will hit many brick walls.

Your credibility with larger companies is usually shaky at best. But once you master the art - on a smaller scale - your skills and credibility will lead you to larger and larger JV partners.

If you approach companies that are around your size (or similar traffic ranking) and smaller, your chance of success is so much higher. In fact, many smaller companies have never even been approached by potential joint venture partners. So here you come along and tell them you want to join forces with them - if their excitement of being approached doesn't get them, your JV proposal sure will...! (We will reveal the ultimate JV proposal in a minute).

Common mistakes made with JV marketing:

Here is a list of common mistakes made when small business owners try to set up joint venture deals.

1. They ask the company to sell their product without keeping in mind "what's in it for the potential joint venture partner." Unless you're approaching companies like Wal-Mart or Kmart, your potential joint venture partner will be far more open if you can offer him some exposure to your customers in return. If selling to a larger distribution company like Kmart (I've been able to sell to Kmart in the past), they will want to know what kind of promotional backing you provide to move the product off their shelves.

2. They offer too small a commission on the sale of the product. I will rarely market another company's product if the commission is below 30%. It's just not worth it. If you want to encourage your potential JV

partner to endorse you, you'd better make it worth his while.

3. They don't follow-up. Most people quit on the first email. And although the email we have crafted below almost always gets a response, we still follow-up. It's about building a relationship.

4. They don't make the joint venture proposal personal enough. Constant bombardment of spam and other impersonal emails allow personalized emails to shine in a crowded market.

5. They target the wrong joint venture partner: Although it's important to JV with companies outside of your immediate market, it's still important to keep it somewhat related. When I say 'related' - I'm referring to a common customer. Don't try JV with a company that has an unsuited target market.

8 Steps to setting up JVs with an 87% success rate.

1. Start by setting up mini JVs with SMALLER businesses than yours. Everyone goes straight after the big deals. That's like trying to scuba dive before you can even tread water. You will need the experience and the success stories. A simple truth is - Stories sell. Testimonials sell. If you don't have any, setting up JVs with smaller businesses is the way to get them. You can usually set up these kinds of JVs without any previous successes.

You only need a few small success stories to give you the kind of credibility to land larger deals. The fastest way to collect success stories is to set up a bunch of smaller deals.

2. Follow-up with examples of success stories. Like selling a product, you need to sell potential JV partners. Success stories and "name dropping" (where you mention someone's name, usually a well known name), will give you instant credibility. We recently landed a great JV deal by name dropping some well known internet market gurus with whom we had JVed in the past. This was done to close the deal, following our initial email.

3. Use mix-medium sequential follow-ups. What does this mean? You need to follow-up multiple times using different forms of contact. For example, we normally email a few times and then follow up with a phone call, if required.

4. Include your phone number or ask them to email their phone number. Once again this adds credibility to your offer. Remember you are selling here. Your JV proposal is a sales letter.

5. Build a relationship anyway you can. If that means referring them business, go ahead and do it. Send an email telling them that one of your clients is interested in their product and that you are going to recommend he check out their site.

6. Use 3 points of personalization. This means that you include at least 3 points that are personal to them. This will give a far more personal feel to your proposal rather than a spam feel. Some ideas might include:

- Where you found their site

- The name of their product

- Something about their product

- Quote a statement (or a line from an article) somebody made about their site

- Their traffic ranking

- Mention a competitor

- Any relevant information you can pick up by scanning their site.

7. Don't be afraid to straight out ask for your potential JV partner to market, or better yet endorse your product. But build a relationship first.

8. Practice on the small deals until you have the confidence and skills to approach the bigger fish.

The ultimate JV proposal:

On the following page is a copy of the exact JV proposal email that almost always gets us a "yes" (even if that "yes" doesn't come immediately).

Hi [Name],

I found your site on WhereEver.com (they had a little write up on you).

I'm the editor of www.YourWebSite.com, a subscription site on running membership sites.

After taking a look at your website, I know that a lot of my customers would be interested in your [name industry] site. We have thousands of subscribers who are specifically interested in [name niche]. Your [name product] is a perfect match. We would like to do an endorsement mailing to our entire list promoting your [name product or service]. Would you be interested in our endorsement mailing? The endorsement would be in the form of an interview or article as we've found this to generate the best response.

We've been able to generate thousands of dollars in additional revenue for companies with which we cross promote (we recently did this for NameaCompany.com)

Also, we have available (normally only available to our paying subscribers) an online audio recording on "Name of Your Product". This eTape would be a valuable resource to your customers and new sign-ups. It would make a perfect premium to add to your subscription service. As you know, the right premium can dramatically increase sales.

Our eTape comes with a report that links back to our [name your site]. We can embed an affiliate link in the eTape so that anyone who subscribes to our site will yield you an ongoing recurring 30% commission for the life of the subscription. Would you like to add our eTape as a premium to your [name package]?

Looking forward to hearing back from you. If you need to discuss anything over the phone just email me your number and the best time to call.

Warmly,
Ansel Gough
Editor

Follow-up strategies

After sending out the first email, wait a few days and then follow-up with another email. Simply ask your potential partner if they received your first email, and then give an example of a successful deal you have done in the past, and suggest similar results for their business.

If the time comes to make a call (usually to finalize the deal), make sure you go over what was said in the emails and ask the JV partner what his/her thoughts are. Welcome their feedback and help lead them so they feel the idea is also their own (even if it was really yours).

Go after the smaller deals and watch your traffic and sales grow.

Real-Life Case Study #5

New Membership Site Owner 'Blogs' his way to success

"... I would say that 75% - 80% of the traffic comes through the blog. I have also used Google Adwords to supplement the highly ranked blog listing."

Former investment researcher throws in his job to launch his very first membership site. Here's how he did it from the ground up, and how he uses 'blogging' to rank in Google's top 30 - generating over 75% of the site's traffic. Have you tried blogging? If not, this may be one of the easiest ways to rank well in the search engines, for free.

1. Tate, so we can have the opportunity to know you a little better, could you tell us a bit about your background?

I've always been a numbers guy. From the time I was in grade school, math and science seemed to come easier for me than the other subjects. However, I enrolled in college not knowing what I wanted to study or what I wanted to do for a living... and that continued through most of college! It wasn't until the final couple of years in college that I discovered the stock market and became fascinated with the way it operated.

It encompassed many of the things I had learned in college... mathematics, economics and psychology.

I read financial magazines and studied the markets by sifting through the internet, but it wasn't until I picked up an Investors Business Daily for the first time that I became really interested in learning how the market works and how to be a successful investor.

By reading IBD and books by William O'Neil, the market began to make sense to me and I wanted to learn more. The more I learned, the more I realized that there were two types of investors. Those who follow the advice of brokers and the conventional advice of Wall Street and those who are enjoying amazing success by doing what works. I spent many nights and Sunday afternoons reading about the methods that work. They all have something in common... their contradiction of conventional investing wisdom.

As my investing "hobby" evolved, it became clear to me that helping others invest is how I wanted to make a living. However, it was important to me to do so on an independent basis using strategies that worked. I was fortunate to get the chance to work as a researcher for one of the top independent investing advisory services around, CANSLIM.net.

I enjoyed following the markets and steering others in the direction of investment success by sharing what I've learned over the years. The next step for me was creating a site of my own, which would offer a tremendous challenge and the creative freedom that I craved.

I decided to give up my position there and just go for it. You only live once, right?

I envisioned a site where investors could learn about a proven investment strategy (with a few modifications of my own) and profit on their own or follow my recommendations and learn from the detailed analysis of featured stocks on a day- to -day basis. In creating the site it was important that it be easily negotiable and void of unnecessary clutter and an overabundance of advertisements screaming buy me, buy me.

2. Well, you sure threw yourself into the project. Can you tell us about your new membership site SelfInvestors.com?

The site is an independent investment advisory service for those interested in investing their own money.

With the advent of the Internet, low commissions, elaborate tracking systems and valuable information once available only to professionals, is now available to everyone, which has levelled the playing field and blurred the lines between amateur and professional investors.

I think people are beginning to realize that they can perform better than a stockbroker... after all, nobody cares more about their money than you do!

I use an investing method based on one of the most successful investing methods ever devised called CANSLIM, developed by William O'Neill. In creating the site, it was important to provide tools/features for investors of all experience levels and to do so in a way so that members can implement a successful strategy in just a few minutes every day.

3. What did you do to research the idea, to make sure that it was viable?

To be honest, I didn't do much research beforehand in terms of what kind of demand for a service like this would be. I did know who my competition was and what kind of service they offered.

4. So you did/do understand the market?

Yes.

Over the years I had used many of them. After looking at the competition and working for the most successful site (using the CANSLIM method of investing), I had a pretty good idea what was currently available for this particular style of investing and how I could improve upon that.

I realized that the site I worked for had a couple thousand members from all over the world and figured if I could capture 10% of their success, I would consider the site a success. I guess you could say I just jumped in with both feet and went for it, knowing that I would have to come up with something unique and improve on what was currently available.

What I probably should have done, is hit the discussion boards to get an idea of what investors are looking for in a service like this and if they would be interested. Set up an online poll and form an online focus group [many forums allow you to do this].

5. Tate, you've only recently launched your site. How well are you doing so far?

While I would like to be able to sit here and say I've got members signing up left and right and am generating thousands of dollars in my first few months, that is not the case as yet.

This is a highly competitive field and it takes time to make a name for yourself. I will admit that it has been much more difficult to get people to pay for the service than I had anticipated. However, currently I have 100 free members and 11 paying members.

6. Well, you've converted 10% of your free members into paying subscribers. That's a high conversion rate. You're off to a good start. How have you been acquiring your subscribers?

Nearly all of my subscribers come through Google in two ways. A related blog and Google Adwords. Why use a blog?

i). Gain credibility through informative articles/lessons.

ii). It's much easier to get ranked in Google with the use of a blog and your information is indexed much faster (I use typepad.com, which apparently is very Google friendly).

iii). It is much easier to get related blogs to link to your blog (you're not competing for customers!). Since blogs typically have high page ranks, so will yours in time. Essentially, you've just created another highly relative, highly ranked site (your blog) to link to your pay site. So now you've also increased the rank of your pay site too!

iv). Free advertising - plug your own site within the articles (without going overboard of course).

It took less than a week to get a blog up, write a couple of posts and achieve a top ten ranking in Google for my targeted keyword which is CANSLIM (acronym for style of investing). I realize that it may not be possible to achieve instant success like this for other keywords, but it is certainly worth a shot.

So here's the process in a nutshell:

a). Gauge the difficulty of getting ranked in Google for a particular keyword by using the following tool:
http://www.searchguild.com/difficulty/

b). Sign up for a typepad blog at www.typepad.com

c). Make sure your keyword appears in the name of your blog.

d). Use the keyword as often as possible without overdoing it. Use in the names of categories, titles of posts, and in the body of the posts.

e). Submit your blog to all the blog search engines. There are about 10 main ones - do a search in Google for "blog search" or "blog directory."

Here are a few to get you started:

www.blogsearchengine.com

www.daypop.com

www.bloogz.com

www.blogarama.com

f). Seek out other blogs in your field (only those that relate to your information and have high page rank) and introduce yourself. Ask if they wouldn't mind linking to you.

g). Watch your Google rank soar!

h). Begin to mention how your membership site will help your readers in a post here and there. You don't want to turn it into a sales page or you'll irritate readers.

That's about it! I would say that 75% - 80% of the traffic comes through the blog. I have also used Google Adwords to supplement the highly ranked blog listing.

I know that Google Adwords can appear on related sites and even other search engines, reaching an audience, which I would not have reached with the blog alone. My current focus has been mostly on investors who are using the CANSLIM method of investing or who are interested in using this method. It is a niche market, but a fairly large one. At some point I will work on targeting other types of investors and try and "sell" them on the approach that I use.

7. What kind of promotions have you been testing?

I haven't done much in the way of promotions yet. I just recently switched from a money back guarantee to a 10 day free trial. It's too soon to gauge the effectiveness of the free trial.

I did install a tell-a-friend program that rewards people who have the most referrals with a free membership. I'll look into other promotional ideas in the future, but I'm still focused on improving the service and bringing in traffic.

8. Did you do your own site design or did you have someone do it for you?

Most of the site was put together by me using trial and error (lots of error!) and reading a few books. I started with a purchased template and made modifications from there, using Frontpage.

As time went on I became aware of the limitations of Frontpage and had to purchase separate programs for menu navigation, pop up windows, page protection, etc. to achieve the results I was looking for.

Recently I've been working to upgrade the look and layout of the premium service, for which I decided to hire a professional. I discovered a great site where web site owners can get in touch with affordable programmers all over the world (www.getafreelancer.com).

I had to try a few different programmers to find one that was experienced, reliable and professional, but it was well worth it. I would be happy to recommend a few names if anyone is interested.

9. Do you have many strategic alliances or joint ventures that bring high volume traffic? If so, how do you go about putting together a joint venture?

This is an area that I have yet to explore. I'm still very busy improving/modifying the premium service to get it to the point where I am 100% satisfied.

As soon as that is done, I will begin to explore partnership opportunities. I have been contacted by a few website owners who asked me to sell their product for them, in exchange for a commission. But I am more interested in a joint venture where both parties work to promote each other's service.

I do have plans to work with an employee of the site I worked for previously who is creating a portal site for CANSLIM investing where articles can be posted. This should increase exposure and credibility and would work more as an affiliate partnership rather than a joint venture.

Commissions will be paid out should I receive paying members from this partnership.

10. What software do you use to manage your membership subscribers?

I spent a ton of time researching this area since it is critical to automating your business. In all my research I was surprised at how few options were available for customer management software.

It became clear that this is a field that is still maturing and has a long way to go.

I did find one program that emerged as a clear winner in customer management software and this was aMember Pro. I know you use this Ansel, as well as many other web site owners who use your site. I really don't believe that there is anything else out there that is worth considering. The tech support you receive is worth the program several times over and I don't know where I'd be without this program.

Before I go into payment processors, I'd like to backtrack a bit and mention that it is somewhat critical for website owners to use a Linux/Unix server for hosting their site. I have found that 90% of the best software/scripts are written for open source Linux platform, including aMember Pro. When I first began to build the site I was hosted on a Windows server, but switched to a Linux server when I began to realize that there were very few options for the Windows platform.

Ok, payment processors - this was an area that caused me a great deal of frustration. Again, I spent many hours researching this area and came to the conclusion that there is no single 3rd party payment processor that contains all of the important features (quick processing, recurring billing, free trials, check processing and affordability).

One solution would be to avoid the 3rd party solutions and get a merchant account, but that doesn't make much sense and may not be possible for a business just starting out.

So, what to do? I use a combination of Paypal.com and 2Checkout.com which has been adequate.

Paypal is very close to becoming a complete payment solution. If they were to allow recurring credit card processing without a PayPal account, there would be no need for any other solution.

In order to allow recurring credit card processing, I've been using 2Checkout which has its limitations. For one, they don't offer the option to allow a free trial that bills automatically when the trial is over. There are also some issues with passing notification of a payment to other programs (such as an affiliate program), which makes it difficult to automate affiliate pay-outs. However, they do process payments quickly and are affordable.

11. Have you tested various pricing levels to find the best combination?

I haven't done any testing in this area yet. Initially, I have used pricing similar to my competitors, but will probably increase the price after upgrades are made and additional features are added.

What's important to me, is not the quantity of subscribers, but the quality. I am genuinely interested in working with investors who are eager to learn about investing and who are interested in working with me to help create a site that fits all of their needs.

12. What kind of premiums do you offer and have you tested different premiums to see if it increases response rates?

In creating the premium service, it was important for me to offer something to investors of all experience levels.

I offer a model portfolio that allows members to see the CANSLIM method of investing in action as well as a "Breakout Tracker" which is a database of stocks ranked according to fundamental and technical analysis.

It allows experienced investors to find the best opportunities the market currently offers, very quickly. Recently I added a Weekly Stock Watch that focuses on a few of these opportunities by providing a detailed technical analysis of each stock. It's designed to get you ready for the week ahead.

13. Have the improvements increased response rate?

It's difficult to say at this point, since the changes were made recently. I have had some very positive feedback from existing members.

14. With that been said - do you feel it's important to offer subscribers something with which they can interact?

I think this is important. At some point I would like to implement a discussion board, but right now I just feel I don't have enough members to make it worthwhile.

15. Although it's only early stages for your membership site, how is your retention? Is there anything that you do in particular to keep subscribers coming back and renewing or keeping their subscriptions?

So far retention has been very good (probably around 75%). When a member cancels I always try and find out why so that I can find out more about who is using the service and how it can be improved.

For users of the free trial that number is much lower (closer to 25%). The key to retaining customers in this particular business is investing performance. If my investing suggestions don't help make my members money, they're not going to continue to sign up. It's as simple as that.

I also believe that customer service is also very important to customer retention. My site is one of the first to offer Live Chat, which is faster than email and more convenient than phone support. When a customer has a question about the service or investing in general, I always make sure I respond in less than 24 hours with a detailed, thoughtful answer.

I want customers to feel like they are important, which they are.

16. What kind of strategy do you use to separate yourself from your competitors?

There are a few ways I try and separate myself from competitors.

As a new site, it's important to gain credibility and I try and do that through the use of the blog, which I mentioned earlier.

Posting informative articles that provide lessons and highlight top stocks is important in doing this.

Using a database of hand picked stocks, all stocks that make it into the database are looked at by me. Some use a mechanical screen, which is never as discriminating and accurate.

For this particular style of investing it is difficult for a computer to find the right buy point on a stock. It is a lot of work, but provides a high quality database of stocks. I use an elaborate tracking system. I have been honing it for a couple of years to keep track of around 600 of the fastest growing companies in the world.

When these stocks are getting ready to break out, they are added to the database. Another way I separate myself from competitors is by posting a model portfolio, which is run like a trading diary. Members know when I make the trade, why I made the trade, how the trade is doing and if the stock will be sold.

I don't know of any competitor who tracks his performance in such detail.

I incorporate feedback from members when making improvements. I make sure that members know this is their service and changes will be made until they are completely satisfied.

As I mentioned earlier, using Live Chat is another customer service option that only I am offering.

17. What have you found to be the best way to convert traffic into paying customers?

I don't really know what the best way is at this time because I haven't been implementing a split testing system to test each change.

There are many important pieces to that puzzle, like your sales pitch, listing credentials, offering a free trial, testimonials, etc. This is an area that I definitely need to work on. Once the upgrades are completed I'll work on tweeking and testing to increase conversion rates.

18. What kind of conversion rate do you have for your site? (Unique visitors to paying customers)

Conversion rates are fairly low in this business due to the tremendous amount of competition. For paying members my conversion is under .5% and around 8% for the free market report.

19. What would be the most important thing you would say to someone trying to start and promote his own membership site (especially from someone who's just started earning his first stream of recurring income)?

Most importantly, you'd better be passionate about your business and be ready to work hard. While success can be had, it's not as easy as it's often made out to be. Of course, using sites like this one can eliminate much of the headache others have gone through in their journey.

There have been times when I would get discouraged and then received an email from a member saying how much he appreciates the service. It keeps me positive and keeps me going each day. Rather than focusing on where I should be at a certain point, I try and focus on how far I've come. Along the way, try to appreciate what you've accomplished rather than where you should be.

CHAPTER 19

Conclusion: What membership website will you start?

Running a successful membership site has allowed me to quit my job, indulge in my interests, travel and work from home, whilst spending every day with my beautiful wife and daughter. For me, it's the perfect business. Anyone can start and run this business model.

There are 4 key elements to always keep in mind before starting your endeavor.

1. **Target the right market.** Find a market that is passionate about a subject (and that you are passionate about), and then build your membership site around it. There are so many topics from which to choose. Doing a keyword search will reveal what people are searching for online. You can know before you even launch a membership site if there's a viable market.

2. **Make it unique.** Ideally potential subscribers shouldn't be able to find the same information elsewhere for free online. Your job is to search online

(and in some case offline) for content, and provide it in a convenient manner for your subscribers. Being unique could just mean having exclusive interviews with experts in your field. If you've done the interview, then that's unique. Finding experts (and even famous people) to interview is not hard. In fact, as your site grows in popularity they are likely to contact you. This situation gives you a two-fold advantage. It gives you credibility or an endorsement, and it gives you exclusive content. Of course your exclusive content may be from your own specialized knowledge!

3. **Finding Subscribers.** If you've started off targeting the right market, then finding traffic and subscribers aren't as difficult as some people believe. The best methods for generating quality traffic to your website as discussed in this book include: Pay-per-click search engine marketing, Internet joint venture marketing, Ezines (online newsletters), affiliate programs, and viral marketing.

4. **Add tools or services.** To enhance your membership site try including simple software, tools, ebooks, resources, etc. as a give-away. These can usually be found for free or at a very low cost online.

The exciting thing is, you can take your hobby, specialized knowledge or profession and turn it into a profitable membership site. Your challenge will be finding exclusive content. You can start it part time – something I did myself, while working a full time job. As your subscriptions increase, you can plan on a full-time career in your area of interest.

What membership site will you start?

Ansel E. Gough

MemberSmart™ BuilderPro

Click 'n Build Your Membership Site, in Minutes

FREE training DVD Included with software

Don't have time or don't know how to design a membership site? Our software will do it for you! Using a proprietary wizard, **MSB Pro** (MemberSmart™ Builder Pro) will simply ask you questions and let you choose a design from our library. Then with a click of the button, it will instantly build your custom membership site before your eyes.

Paying to have a membership site professionally designed (unless you build it yourself) could cost several thousand dollars. Our software will do the same job, within minutes, at less than 10% of the cost and you can build as many membership sites as you like.

MemberSmart™ Builder will also manage your entire membership site, allowing you to make design changes, add articles and manage content all at the click of a button.

Software features:

- Instant website design using question based wizard
- Library of designs to choose from
- Library of graphics to choose from
- Modify actual design code (for advanced users)
- Content and article management
- Automatic archiving of articles
- Comes with exclusive password protection software
- Accept PayPal and Credit Card payments from new subscribers
- Installs directly onto your computer
- Works on Mac & PC
- Includes FREE "Getting Started" tutorial DVD

Free trial download:

To download a free trial version, just go to:

www.MemberSmartBuilder.com

www.ingramcontent.com/pod-product-compliance
Lightning Source LLC
Chambersburg PA
CBHW051235050326
40689CB00007B/923